CHRISTMAS IN HOLLYBROOK

Amish Romance

BRENDA MAXFIELD

Tica House Publishing

Sweet Romance that Delights and Enchants!

Personal Word from the Author

Dearest Readers,

Thank you so much for choosing one of my books. I am proud to be a part of the team of writers at Tica House Publishing who work joyfully to bring you stories of hope, faith, courage, and love. Your kind words and loving readership are deeply appreciated.

I would like to personally invite you to sign up for updates and to become part of our **Exclusive Reader Club**—it's completely Free to join! We'd love to welcome you!

Much love,

Brenda Maxfield

VISIT HERE to Join our Reader's Club and to Receive Tica House Updates:

www.ticahousepublishing.subscribemenow.com

Chapter One

> And be ye kind to one another, tenderhearted, forgiving one another, even as God for Christ's sake hath forgiven you.
>
> — EPHESIANS 4:32 KJV

Sadie Verkler stood at the warming stove, holding her hands out to soak up the heat. There was a decided nip in the air even though she'd poked at the banked fire to get it going over an hour before. She glanced out the window through the frosty panes.

Well, it was early December in Ohio. This kind of cold snap was to be expected.

"Child, you all packed?" Sadie's grandmother, Henrietta Verkler, asked. "The van will be here soon to pick you up."

"I don't want to go," Sadie said without thinking. She cringed. At nineteen years of age, she sounded like a petulant child. "Sorry," she muttered.

"It'll be fine. You'll see. And your *mamm* will be right glad to have you home." Henrietta shook her head with a wry grin and a chuckle. "Imagine. Expecting a new *boppli* at her age."

In truth, Sadie had a hard time reconciling that fact herself. Even though many Amish women bore children well into their forties, Sadie had never expected it to happen with her mother. Goodness, her youngest sibling, Matilda was already nine years old. There would be quite a gap between her and this new one.

"I'm glad you'll be there to help," Henrietta went on. "Them boys are busy with men's work and won't be a lick of help to your *mamm*. Lizzie and Matilda will be of help, for sure and for certain, but you're the one your *mamm* needs."

"I know. And I'm glad to help. Truly, I am. I just don't want to leave you." Sadie had been with her grandmother for nearly two years, ever since Henrietta had tripped and broken her leg. Her leg was better now, of course, but Sadie had been content to stay on.

Sadie had never admitted to her grandmother the main reason she had been so quick to come live with her and help. She shuddered, trying not to think on it. Nothing good came from dwelling on a broken heart. It had taken months for her yearning to fade into a dull ache. And now, Sadie preferred not to think of it at all. But it was hard, knowing she was going right back to Hollybrook, Indiana. Right back to where Peter Wyse lived.

She'd never asked her mother about Peter's wedding. Never asked anyone in Hollybrook how he was surviving the death of his young wife. When Sadie learned of Eloise's death, she had been stunned into silence for hours. How could a twenty-year-old simply *die?* Eloise hadn't been sick. She hadn't suffered. There had been no clue and no hint of any trouble health-wise. She'd simply bent over to tie her shoe one day and died.

Sadie's mother had written her to say that *Englisch* doctors thought there had been something wrong with Eloise's heart from birth, but of course, Peter wouldn't agree to any sort of examination. The very thought of *Englisch* doctors cutting into Eloise to figure out the whys was inconceivable. So, Eloise Gundy Wyse had been swiftly buried and mourned.

Sadie didn't know how Peter was doing. Was he all right? Was he eating properly? Was he sleeping? It had been nearly a year ago now, for he and Eloise had only been married a few months before the tragedy.

Had he adjusted?

Such questions were the reason Sadie tried not to think of

him. It was too disturbing. Too raw. Such thoughts plunged her back into the past where she didn't want to live.

Besides, she'd moved on, hadn't she? She was now smitten with Aaron Roggi, and he lived right there in Ainesburg, Ohio. During the last month, he'd driven her home twice from Youth Singings. He owned a fine courting buggy with a heater in it, of all things. But oh, how pleasant it was in the cold winter air. Never in Sadie's life had she ridden in a buggy with a heater. In truth, she hadn't even known they existed, but she was spoiled now, that was for sure and for certain.

Sadie always made a concerted effort never to compare Aaron with Peter. What good would come of it? If she didn't feel that same tug, that same pull on her heart that she'd had with Peter, she just needed to be patient. It would come. She closed her eyes, but Aaron's image was quickly crowded out by Peter's. How well she remembered Peter's eyes as he looked into hers. They were such a deep blue that Sadie sometimes fancied them almost purple. Peter's eyes had a spark in them, too, a twinkle of sorts that made him always seemed amused by something. In truth, Aaron's eyes seemed ordinary and unimpressive next to Peter's.

Peter used to give her a happy feeling. Like if she stayed by his side, life would be fun and rewarding—not just an endless series of chores and work and rules and judgements.

She shivered and opened her eyes. Goodness, but where her

mind went sometimes. Surely such thoughts were not pleasing to God.

"Did you?" Henrietta was asking.

Sadie gave a start. "Did I what, *Mammi*?"

"Did you pack yourself some food for the trip? There's some left-over meatloaf that would make a *gut* sandwich."

"*Jah.* I already made one. I made one for you, too. It's on the top shelf in the refrigerator." Sadie took a step closer to where her grandmother sat at the kitchen table. "Why don't you come with me? I don't like leaving you here."

"*Ach,* child. We've gone over and over this. Ainesburg is my home. I've lived here my whole life. Your *daadi* built this house. He died in it, and I plan to do the same."

"But you could be with us. And you could help us with the new *boppli.*"

"I ain't needed to help with the new *boppli,* and you know it. You're going to be all the help your *mamm* needs. *Nee,* child. This is my place."

"I'll come back after the *boppli's* born. I promise, I will."

"You'll do no such thing. Your *mamm* will still need you for a *gut* while."

"But once the *boppli's* born, my sisters can be all the help needed. You know that, *Mammi*. I can come back."

Henrietta smiled, her thin lips pulling up at the corners. "I haven't asked before, and I hesitate to do it now. But, you have a young fella here, *ain't so?*"

Sadie felt her cheeks flush.

"Never mind," Henrietta went on. "Those red cheeks of yours are telling enough."

"But Christmas is going to be here before we know it," Sadie tried again. "I don't want you in this house alone on Christmas. It ain't right."

Henrietta patted Sadie's hand. "It's sweet how you fuss over me. I'm an old woman, Sadie. I can be by myself on Christmas. Besides, there will be the program at the school, you know. And I expect I'll be asked over by the Bellams."

"But you should be with us." Sadie sighed, not liking the image of her grandmother waking up alone on Christmas Day. But she also knew how stubborn her grandmother could be. If she said she was staying put, then she was staying put.

"I'll come back for Christmas, then. And afterward, I'll go back to help *Mamm*."

"Sadie Verkler, I won't be hearing of it. I won't be taking you away from your family for another Christmas. You've already spent two of them with me."

"You know, *Mammi*, I can be as stubborn as you are."

Henrietta laughed, and her eyes turned misty. Sadie saw it and a pang went through her heart. She really did prefer to stay, and not only so she could avoid seeing Peter. She loved being with her grandmother there in Ainesburg.

A crunch of gravel sounded from outside. With a sinking heart, Sadie peered through the window and saw a van approaching the front porch.

"He's here, *ain't so?*" Henrietta announced. "Get on out there. Don't make him wait."

Sadie faced her, tears now pricking her own eyes. "You're sure, *Mammi?* You're sure you'll be all right?"

Henrietta nodded. "Go on with you." She waved her hand in exaggerated dismissal. "Get out of here."

Sadie leaned down and gave her a quick hug. Henrietta's tiny frame felt fragile in her arms. Everything in Sadie screamed at her to stay, but she knew it wasn't her choice. Her father had sent for her—she was needed at home. Just as she had been needed there in Ohio two years before.

As she gave her grandmother a last long look, she wondered whether she would ever really be able to make her own choices in life. So far, it hadn't worked out that way very often. But she could hardly ignore or disobey a direct mandate from her father.

Even though she fussed with Henrietta like she had a choice —she didn't. She had to go back to Hollybrook, Indiana.

Chapter Two

Sadie closed the door behind her and hurried down the porch steps. The driver, a Mennonite man named George they often used, stood outside the back passenger door. He slid it open for her.

"How are you, Sadie?"

She nodded and smiled, not trusting her voice to speak. At least not yet. He must have sensed her sadness, for he said nothing further until they were leaving the city limits of Ainesburg. Then he looked at her from his rear-view mirror.

"You must be mighty happy to be seeing your family again."

She swallowed and cleared her throat. "*Jah.* It's been a while."

"I should say it has. A good six months or so."

It had been a whole lot longer than six months, but she didn't feel like correcting him. In truth, she'd only been back once, and that was a quick trip of only three days. Three days in which she kept close to home, not venturing out to see anyone. But now if she was moving back, she could hardly hole up in the house and never see a soul.

Well, never see Peter Wyse, to be specific.

How was it possible that she could continue to harbor feelings for a boy who had rejected her? And two years ago, for goodness sake? It seemed absurd. Impossible. She reached over and patted her suitcase. Inside was a letter from Aaron. She was tempted to open up her suitcase right then and there and re-read it. Perhaps that would help her ignore the thoughts of her old beau. But what would the driver think? It seemed awfully silly to be digging through her suitcase for a letter that she'd only just packed the night before.

She shook her head in disgust at herself and gazed out the window. She would never get used to how the scenery sped by in a blur in a motor car. A person hardly had the chance to see something before it was torn from view and something else replaced it. She surely liked the convenience and the warmth of modern cars, but she deeply preferred the rhythmic motion of a horse and buggy.

During the rest of the trip, George offered comments now and again, but it was mostly silent. He offered to stop and take a short break at the state border, but Sadie preferred to just continue on. Stopping at the border wasn't going to change anything.

"Can you direct me to your farm?" he asked as they neared Hollybrook. "I didn't plug your address into my cell, but I figured you could steer me easy enough."

Hating the tremor in her voice, Sadie gave running directions until they were pulling into her drive. Being December, she didn't see anyone out and about. Likely, chores were finished and they were all huddled around the warming stove in the front room. George pulled up to the porch just as the front door of the house burst open.

Lizzie and Matilda came tumbling out, their blue eyes alight with excitement.

"Your sisters?" George asked, coming to a complete stop.

"Jah." Despite her misgivings, Sadie's heart beat more quickly at the sight of them. My, but how they'd grown. She got out of the van and they rushed to her, nearly bowling her over.

"You're finally here!" Lizzie said, nuzzling Sadie's arm.

"I'm here." Sadie smiled.

Matilda pulled on her sleeve. "Come on inside."

"Wait. I have to grab my bag."

"Let me know if you need my services again," George interrupted them. "You have my number?"

"*Jah.* Thank you." Sadie said. Although she was happier than she'd thought she'd be to see her sisters, she still wished that this was only a short stay. She still wished that she could return to her grandmother's by Christmas.

"I got your bag," Lizzie said, holding the suitcase with both hands and awkwardly heading for the porch steps. The suitcase bopped along before her, slapping back to hit her legs at every step.

"Then, shall we go?" Sadie asked, following Lizzie.

Before they got to the door, it opened again and Bonnie Verkler stood before them. "Goodness, but it's right fine to see you, daughter," she said, her usual full, mellow voice lower than Sadie remembered. Her mother's eyes looked tired, and it was hard to miss the dark circles beneath them. There was a sallow tinge to her cheeks, too, unlike the usual stereotypical glow of an expectant mother.

"Hello, *Mamm*. I'm glad to see you, too."

"Come in quick. It's awful cold out today."

Sadie and her sisters hurried inside. Sadie paused for a moment after she shut the door, letting the smell and sounds of home sink into her. It all seemed so wonderfully familiar, yet strangely different from the smells of *Mammi's* house. Sadie would have to get used to it all over again. Her father gave her a nod from the front room, and her brothers Mark and Roger grinned at her and hollered their greetings.

"You hungry, child?" *Mamm* asked.

"*Nee*. I had a sandwich on the way. Besides, you sit on down. I'm here to help, remember?"

Bonnie chuckled. "So you are. But this household needs more than one person to run it."

"Mamm," cried Lizzie, indignant. "I help. And so does Matilda."

"For sure and for certain, you do," *Mamm* replied. "I declare, I couldn't do it without you."

"Well, now you have me, too."

"How's *Mammi?*" Matilda asked. "I wanted her to come home with you."

Sadie patted Matilda's *kapp*. "I tried. Truly, I did. But she won't budge from Ohio."

Mamm tsked her tongue against her teeth. "She's a stubborn one, your *dat's mamm*."

"That she is." Sadie pulled out a chair from the dining table for her mother. "Sit down. Do you want some tea?"

"*Nee*," *Mamm* said, sinking into the chair with a heavy sigh. "I have to visit the bathroom every ten minutes as it is."

"Old Mae been?" Sadie asked, wondering if her mother had seen the district's medicine woman.

"She comes every week," Matilda announced. "Says *Mamm* is doing fine, just needs to rest some."

Sadie nodded, relieved that Old Mae was so involved. "So that's what we're going to make sure of, *ain't so?*" She looked at both her sisters.

They nodded solemnly, and Lizzie set Sadie's suitcase on the bench. "Want me to take this up for you?"

"I can do it," Sadie said.

"We, uh, well, we changed things around a bit," *Mamm* explained.

"What do you mean?"

"We didn't see any use in wasting your bedroom when you wasn't here," she continued. "Lizzie has been using your room. Matilda's on her own in the furthest room. But now, we've had to get a nursery prepared. We can move Lizzie back—"

Before she'd hardly gotten the words out, Lizzie was groaning.

"Elizabeth," *Mamm* warned.

Lizzie looked momentarily ashamed, but she recovered quickly enough. "Can't Sadie move in with Matilda? I'm sure they'd like to share a room."

Sadie raised her brow. She was ready to agree, for after all, she was the one who left nearly two years ago. It would be awfully presumptuous to assume she'd get her old room back. But before she could say so, their mother made herself quite clear.

"That may be true, Elizabeth Verkler. But your sister is older by some years, and as such, she gets the privilege of the room. Now, if you'd like to bed down in the nursery, that can be arranged. Then, when this *boppli* comes, you can be the first one to tend to her. Or him." She gave Lizzie a stern look. "So, which is it?"

Lizzie let out her breath. "I'll be sleeping with Matilda," she said. "But *Mamm*, I'll be happy to get up with the *boppli* sometimes. Really."

Mamm laughed. "I believe you, child. Well. Now, that's settled. Why don't you two run off and let me catch up with my eldest?"

Both the girls ran off, and Sadie sat down opposite her mother. "How are you feeling?"

Mamm tipped her head and sighed. "In truth, I'm tired. I'm so glad your *dat* sent for you." She gave Sadie a piercing look. "Did you want to come home?"

Sadie hesitated. She hardly wanted to lie to her mother. "I wanted to see you," she answered honestly. "But I hated to leave *Mammi.* And I really don't want her alone on Christmas."

"She could come here."

"You said it yourself. She's stubborn."

"So, you want to go back." The words were spoken frankly, without accusation.

Sadie felt badly that they were true, but there it was.

"You don't have to cushion my feelings. You've been in Ohio for two years. It's only natural that your life is there now."

Sadie reached out and clasped her mother's hand, relieved that she understood.

"And is there a young man?"

Sadie blanched. Such things weren't discussed. Her mother burst into laughter.

"*Ach.* You should see your face. What's his name?"

Sadie only hesitated for a moment. "He's a farmer there. We, well, I don't know if we're courting seriously or not." Although having Aaron's letter tucked safely in her suitcase indicated as much. But being back in Hollybrook, being back in her childhood home, brought the memory of Peter back to her more strongly than she'd hoped.

"I always wanted to talk to you about something," her mother was saying. "Now, I understand all about what's talked about and what isn't. Land's sake, girl, I've lived over forty years. And, the Lord *Gott* knows, I've kept quiet on this for months and months. So, even though I know it's frowned upon and discouraged, I am going to ask you now..."

Sadie tensed, fearing where her mother was going with such talk.

"Were you in love with Peter Wyse when you left?"

Sadie sucked in a loud breath, surprised by her mother's bold question, and even more surprised by her mother's insight. She'd thought she'd hidden her feelings well.

Bonnie Verkler shook her head sadly. "So, it's as I feared. It's written all over your face. I'm sorry. At the time, I thought it puzzling that you jumped so quickly at the chance to help *Mammi*." She held up her hand as if to stop Sadie's objection. "Oh, I know you love your *Mammi* and would do anything for her. But I always thought you'd come home, or at least not be so eager to shed your life here. It didn't add up for a teenage girl. You had dear friends here, and I knew you were seeing someone. At least for a while. I noticed how you'd come home late some evenings..."

She leaned forward and whispered to Sadie. "You were with Peter, *ain't so?*"

Sadie gulped past the rapidly growing lump in her throat. "*Jah*," she whispered.

"It must have hurt you something fierce when he married Eloise."

Hurt her something fierce? Sadie closed her eyes, not wanting to remember it.

"*Ach,* I'm sorry," her mother went on. "What am I thinking, bringing all this up?"

"It's ... it's all right," Sadie said, opening her eyes and focusing back on her mother. "Would you like to take a nap, *Mamm*? You're looking pale."

"A nap? What would your *dat* be thinking if I took a nap. *Nee*." She stood. "I'm thinking that it's about time to get supper started."

Sadie stood also, and pushed her mother back down. "I'll be getting supper on the table. Me and Lizzie and Matilda. You're going to get some rest, just like Old Mae said."

Chapter Three

Peter Wyse wandered through the *daadi haus* he still lived in. Actually, it was his late wife's family *daadi haus*. He should have moved out. And he'd intended to move out more than once, but every time he started to pack up, Eloise's mother would somehow know. She'd leave the big house and come back there to visit him. She'd go on and on about how having Peter still with them kept Eloise's memory alive for her.

And then what could he do?

He had to stay. How could he hurt his in-laws?

But the very reason that Eloise's mother wanted him to stay was the very reason he wanted to leave. Wandering through the small house was like walking through an empty grave. Eloise wasn't there, but all her things were. The first few months had been excruciating. Her scent had remained, along with her things. Everywhere he turned, he could smell her. He kept expecting her to be there, smiling at him, laughing at something he said.

But she wasn't there. She was gone. She was dead.

And he'd had to accept it. They'd barely had six months together as man and wife. Barely enough time to really know each other. Eloise had been such a sweet girl. Fragile. Delicate. Strange how none of them had ever guessed there was something wrong with her heart. He knew that she got out of breath easily. Whenever, she walked through the fields, she would pant. When he'd question it, she would just laugh and say that she needed to eat a bit more—get up her strength.

He hadn't given it enough thought. Maybe if he had, he could have prevented her from dying. He stopped his pacing. Foolish thought. He couldn't have stopped anything. God had called her home. Pure and simple. And it wasn't his place to question it or to question God.

He walked to the kitchen and stood in the middle of the floor as if he were lost. It was past the supper hour. Eloise's mother hadn't invited him over, but he knew he could go to the big house and eat with them—he'd done so often enough. But not every meal. And he didn't like the feeling it gave him sometimes. Like he was a pitiable person who lived off his relatives.

He went to the refrigerator and pulled it open. A ketchup

bottle, some mayonnaise, a partial loaf of bread, and a shriveled apple. He grabbed the bread and took out a slice. He opened a cupboard door and found the peanut butter. He slathered a thick layer onto the bread and sat down at the kitchen table. What a meal.

He *was* pitiable.

Other men learned how to cook, and he supposed he could, too. He aimlessly looked around the adjoining front room. It was tidy enough—he did make sure of that. But it was empty. *Empty.* He took three more huge bites finishing off the slice of bread. He stood up and grabbed his coat from the peg by the front door and went outside.

He sucked in a quick breath at the frigid temperatures. It was dark out, the sun now falling at four-thirty or so every afternoon. He probably should have brought a lantern with him, but he wasn't in the mood to have the Gundy family watch him walk across the lawn and out to the road. They'd wonder where he was headed, and rightly so.

One didn't walk around in the dark for no reason. But that was exactly what he was doing—walking around in the dark for no reason. Only to escape his home. He needed to move out. In the worst way, he needed to move out. He could probably go back to his parents' farm. His old bedroom stood empty. But for some reason, that didn't appeal to him either.

Dear Lord, he was a man without a home. He got to the road

and turned left, wandering in the growing cold without a thought as to where he was going. The frigid air actually felt good to him, slapping at his face, allowing him to feel something besides his own tiresome emotions. This simply couldn't continue. Winter was the hardest. Summer kept him so busy helping Jess Gundy on the farm that it left little time to think. But the winters... He plodded through the days addlebrained.

He drew in a deep breath. He needed to marry again.

His thoughts darted to the days before he proposed to Eloise. He'd been courting Sadie Verkler. Despite his current mood, he grinned. Sadie was fun. Lively. Curious. His jaw tightened. He'd done her wrong. He knew Sadie had wanted to marry him. She was in love with him, and he had been halfway in love with her. No, in truth, he had loved her.

But then, Eloise had begun showing interest. She needed him. Her frail nature and soft-spoken manner had cut straight through his heart. Sadie was strong. But Eloise—now, there was a girl who truly needed a protector—and Peter had stepped up to do the job. He couldn't even put into words what had come over him. He supposed he'd fallen head over heels in love. At the time, that was what he'd thought, anyway. And indeed, he had loved Eloise. Sweet, sweet Eloise.

But lately, when he thought on it, he realized that her need had fed him somehow. Blinded him with importance. Led him into their whirlwind courtship. But he'd always felt guilty about dropping Sadie like that. He wished he would have handled it differently. She deserved so much better.

He could have married Sadie, and they would have been happy. He shook his head. He couldn't be thinking in such a manner. Sadie had left for Ohio shortly after he'd left her. He'd heard it was to take care of her grandmother, and indeed, that was probably partially true. Because at the time, even in his hazy infatuated mind, he'd known that Sadie had left to escape him.

The thought still bothered him, but it had evidently turned out for the best. Sadie was still gone. Still in Ohio. That had to mean she was happy there. She surely wasn't still mourning his loss after so long—she surely wasn't still living there to avoid him. He wasn't that naïve.

He found himself wanting to see her. Wanting to talk with her. Wanting to hear her laugh. Sadie's laughter was contagious, and he smiled at the memory of it.

Ach, what was he doing? She was likely married by now. He'd always avoided any news of Sadie, feeling too guilty to listen.

"I wish you well, Sadie," he whispered into the darkness. He increased his pace, walking harder, breathing deeper, feeling the air slice through his lungs. Maybe it was going to snow. Folks favored a white Christmas, even though it made travel dangerous and miserable.

It was time to go back to his house. By the time he got there, he could read for a bit and then turn in for the night. He never stayed up late, as he didn't enjoy sitting there alone with his thoughts. Bed was the answer. And sleep. A person didn't think when they were asleep.

Chapter Four

Sadie stood inside her old bedroom and looked around. Lizzie had moved the dresser from beside the window to closer to the door. Other than that, everything was the same as the day she'd left. Even the same green and white star quilt covered the bed.

It was as if she'd never been gone. But she had. Everything had changed. Peter had gotten married and was now a widower. Aaron Roggi had started to court her in Ohio. It wasn't lost on Sadie that the main changes she took note of had to do with courtship and love. She opened her suitcase that was lying on the bed. She took out Aaron's letter and sat down at the head of the bed, next to the pillow. She leaned slightly toward the lantern on the bedside table and unfolded the letter.

. . .

Dear Sadie,

I am glad that you'll be of help to your mamm in Hollybrook. It does sound like she needs you there. But I'm hopeful you will return before long.

I am asking if you'd allow me to write you while you're gone. Consider this the first letter of many. Thank you for giving me your address. Surely, you must have figured out why I asked for it. So, the fact that you gave it to me hopefully indicates your agreement to exchange letters. I guess I'll find out soon.

I do love this Christmas season. Work outside has slowed to almost nothing, and everyone stays huddled together by the warming stove. Mamm puts out puzzles for us to work on, and they're a nice way to pass the time.

Will you be returning for Christmas? I know I asked you that earlier, but you weren't sure. I'm wondering if you now know. My three younger sisters are practicing their recitations for the school Christmas program. I tease them, and they get so upset with me. But it is all done in fun.

Please write to me, Sadie. I'm eager to hear how your mamm is and how you are doing over there in Hollybrook.

Your faithful friend,

Aaron

When Sadie had first read his letter, her heart had warmed.

Aaron liked her. He liked her fine, and he was the age when fellows started looking in earnest for a wife. But now, sitting there in her former bedroom and holding his letter, her feelings had changed. She felt a disconnect that was new. She shivered and frowned. What was wrong with her? Why should she feel differently about Aaron's letter just because she'd come home?

But she knew why. Her hand shook as she folded Aaron's letter and returned it to the envelope. She *knew why.* Being back home had plunged her into the past. Plunged her right back into her former feelings.

And all she could think about was Peter Wyse.

She stuck Aaron's letter in the bedside table's drawer and stood up to put away her belongings. It wouldn't take long; she didn't have much. When she hung her last dress on a peg by the door she again stood and gazed about her room.

What was she to do now? Everyone was tucking in for the night, so she could hardly go downstairs and look for something to do. She sighed. She used to keep a few books in the bottom drawer of the dresser. Maybe they were still there and she could read one of them—that would get her mind off things. She knelt on the floor and opened the drawer. She let out a small gasp of pleasure. They were still there. She grabbed the top one, which was *Little Women*. Her mother had raised a brow when she'd selected it from a rack at an *Englisch* drug store years before. But after reading the flap, her mother had given her go-ahead and Sadie had purchased the book.

Now, Sadie ran her hand over the well-worn cover, feeling as though she'd just found an old friend. She changed quickly into her nightgown and then got under her covers and settled in for a nice read. But she couldn't concentrate. She turned up the lantern, increasing the light, but that didn't help. She read out loud to herself in a soft whisper, hoping that would keep her mind on the story.

That didn't help either. Finally, she put the book aside and grabbed the tablet and pencil from the bedside table. She'd write to Aaron. That was what she would do. Surely, that would help her feel closer to him and get Peter off her mind.

Dear Aaron,

I've arrived. Thank you for the letter you sent right before I left Ainesburg. It was sweet of you to write.

My family is well. Mamm is tired, but doing all right. I'm glad I can be here to manage things for her. It will be odd with so many in the family, as I'm used to just Mammi and me.

I would like to return for Christmas. In truth, I plan to. But I haven't shared that news with Mamm an Dat yet. I think it wisest to wait.

Sadie re-read what she had written. It sounded friendly, warm.

At least, she thought so. But she didn't want to write Aaron. She wanted to write Peter. She drew in a sharp breath. What was she thinking? Of course, she couldn't write Peter. Or *could she?* Couldn't she write to Peter and not send the letter?

Her pulse increased at the thought. Yes. She could do that. It might help to get her feelings out. She wouldn't send the letter; she would hide it away there in her bedroom. She'd heard once that writing was a good way to deal with unwanted feelings. And goodness, but she needed to get this ball of confusion out of her heart, for sure and for certain.

She quickly signed her letter to Aaron and folded it, ready for an envelope and stamp in the morning. Then she ripped off another piece of paper and began writing again.

Dear Peter,

I'm back in Hollybrook now. Of course, I don't expect you to know that, which is why I'm telling you. I didn't want to come. Because of you, Peter. Because of you. You hurt me so badly when you dropped me. I had thought that you liked me. Didn't you? How I liked you. Nee. How I loved you. You broke my heart.

When I look back now, I can still feel that young girl's broken heart. I don't really blame you, of course. You were totally free to choose whoever you wanted to court. I had hoped it would be me. And it was for a little while, wasn't it? I loved those times we spent together. I had such dreams. Oh, I was a foolish girl.

But I loved you.

I fear I still do. And I don't want to. You made your choice two years ago. So, loving you now is quite sad, actually. I am ashamed to even admit it, which is why I'm writing it in this letter which will never reach you.

I am so sorry for your loss, Peter. My heart breaks for you. How awful that Eloise died. I can't even imagine how hurt you must have been and maybe still are. She was a nice girl. But then, you know that. You loved her. I'm so sorry.

It's odd to be back home. I feel like time hasn't really passed. Like I'm caught in a spider web and can't pull myself out of it. I'm wriggling and wriggling, but I'm trapped in its sticky threads. I don't want to be here. I want to go back to Ohio to be with Mammi.

Yet part of me wants to see you first. Not necessarily to talk to you or anything, just to see you. I have such an image of you in my head, and I have no idea if you look the same or not. I don't even know if I look the same. Probably not. Two years can seem forever, can't it? Goodness. I just said the opposite earlier. I guess I just want to see if you're all right. I don't want to worry about you.

I don't want to think about you.

Maybe if I see you, I can forget you. And maybe if I see you, I won't feel anything. That's what I am hoping for. To not feel anything except Christian love.

Goodness, but I'm going on and on, aren't I? I guess it doesn't matter since you won't read this. So, really, I suppose I'm writing to myself. Now that is an odd thought.

Love,

Sadie

Sadie didn't know why she signed the letter with the word *love*. Maybe because it was safe to do so. Peter wouldn't see it. Only she would read it. She sighed heavily. She didn't want to know why she signed it that way, and it didn't matter. She folded the letter up tightly, much smaller than the size of a normal envelope and wrote Peter's name on the outside of it. Then she tucked it into the back of the drawer where no one would find it.

With that, she lowered the wick in the lantern, snuffing it out. She scrunched down into the bed, pulling the quilt up to her chin, and waited for sleep to come.

Chapter Five

Peter pulled on his woolen coat.

"You should go," his mother said, straightening her *kapp*.

"*Mamm*, I'm not a youth."

"You're single. That's *gut* enough."

Peter sighed. Sometimes, his mother was exhausting. Now he remembered why he hadn't come straight back home to live after Eloise passed.

"I'm going to tell the Fishers to expect you." Verna Wyse drew herself up to her full height, as if that would strengthen her argument.

"*Mamm*, I don't want to go."

Verna leaned in, her blue eyes spitting fire. "It's just going caroling for an evening. There will be lots of folks there, and not just the younger youth. Besides, you're twenty-two years old—hardly an old man. And you like Christmas carols. You always have."

She was right about that. He did love Christmas carols. But the year before, Christmas had been excruciating. Everyone had tried to be so kind to him, so understanding, which had only made it worse. He wasn't looking forward to Christmas this year for that very fact. Although, he already knew it wasn't going to be as bad. But the loneliness. It tormented him. The way it sometimes gripped his throat made it hard for him to breathe, let alone sing.

"Sadie Verkler is going to be there," his mother added.

Peter froze. Sadie? Was she *back?* His mind spun, and a horrible aching lurched through his heart. When had she come back to Hollybrook?

His mother was studying him, and he forced a neutral expression to his face. His breath had hitched in his chest and he felt a sudden urge to sit down. But he remained standing, not moving. He wanted to question his mother, but he didn't dare. He had no business asking about Sadie Verkler. And he was pretty sure Sadie wouldn't want a thing to do with him.

His mother's eyes had now narrowed, and he could practically hear her thoughts echo through the room.

"Stop," he said curtly.

"I won't stop," she protested. "I saw that look on your face. And don't you think for one moment that I didn't know about you and Sadie. You were sweet on her, *ain't so*? You used to take her driving."

His breath gushed out in a huge sigh. "*Mamm*, leave it alone. Please."

"I won't leave it alone. You need a wife. Sadie is back and you used to like her."

"Well, she doesn't like me," he snapped.

"You don't know that. Who wouldn't like you? You're a fine young man."

He couldn't bear listening to her for one more minute. "I'm leaving," he said, and he pushed out the side door, wishing that he'd brought the pony cart. He was in no mood to walk the mile or so back to his *daadi haus*. But then, maybe the walk would do him good. He pulled up the collar of his coat against the biting wind.

He heard the side door open behind him.

"You're going!" his mother called. "I'm telling the Fishers to expect you!"

He didn't turn around. Instead, he walked toward the road, his stride long and quick. Christmas Caroling. At that moment, he couldn't think of anything he'd less rather do.

Bumbling around with a bunch of teenagers didn't sound remotely fun.

But Sadie... His chest tightened. She was back. That was unexpected news. Was she back to stay? And how could it be that such a pretty girl wasn't being courted. In truth, she likely had a beau. She was probably only back for the holidays. He kicked at a rock on the road sending it spinning into a fallow field. He'd like to see her. There was no denying that. But he'd been telling his mother the truth. He was quite certain Sadie wouldn't want to see him—wouldn't want to have anything to do with him, and rightly so.

He shoved his hands into his pockets and hunched against the wind. It was going to be a long mile back home. He slowed. If he walked the long way, he'd pass right by the Verkler farm. If he was lucky, he'd see Sadie outside. Maybe she'd be running to the hen house or going out to the barn. Didn't the Verklers have goats? He couldn't remember.

Ach, he was being ridiculous. That route would add a good half hour to his walk, and it was freezing cold. But what else did he have to do right then? And walking was good for the heart and lungs, wasn't it? Without thinking further, he turned and headed back to take the long way around. He purposefully didn't dwell on his decision. He simply bent his head into the wind and walked with almost fierce determination.

Chapter Six

"Well, we're going," Sadie's brother Roger announced. "Me and Mark. We can take you with us if you want."

"The Fishers are hosting?" Sadie asked.

"Yeah, and they always have the best food," Mark piped up.

"Wish *I* could go," Lizzie said, sticking out her bottom lip.

"You'll be able to, soon enough," Bonnie Verkler said from the davenport, where she was sitting with her feet up.

"In three more years," Lizzie complained. "That ain't soon enough."

Bonnie laughed at her daughter and then closed her eyes, folding her hands over her protruding stomach.

"Don't matter if you don't want to go, Sadie," Roger said. "Just offering you a ride."

Sadie loved to go Christmas caroling. She wondered fleetingly if Peter would be there, but she decided he wouldn't. As a widower, he wasn't exactly a youth anymore, even though he was single and young. Although, he did like to sing. Sadie grimaced. She didn't know him anymore. For all she knew, he hated singing now.

"What time are you leaving? It's Friday evening, right?"

"*Jah.* We'll hitch up around five-thirty."

Sadie nodded slowly. It would be nice to see her old friends again. Plus, it would give her something to do. "I probably will go. Thanks for asking me."

Roger shrugged and then he and Mark headed off toward the barn to check on the cows.

"Lizzie, can you run get me some tea?" Bonnie asked her middle daughter.

"*Jah, Mamm*. Matilda, come help me."

After the two girls left, Sadie's mother looked at her. "He'll be there, you know."

Sadie didn't have to ask whom she meant. "Maybe," she said softly.

"*Nee.* I reckon he'll be there sure enough." Her mother scrutinized her. "You all right with that?"

"Of course," Sadie said, putting a light tone in her voice. But inside, she wasn't so sure. And she didn't like the way her pulse quickened at the thought.

Late afternoon on Friday, the boys and Sadie bundled up as if preparing for a blizzard.

"Gonna be right cold out there tonight," their mother warned.

"I think some are taking vans to different farms to sing. And then there's some gonna be walking." Mark grinned. "I'm gonna be in a van."

Roger gave him a gentle shove. "I'm thinking the Fishers will be in charge of who goes where. No need to get your hopes up."

Sadie didn't join the conversation. Her mind was fully occupied with the possibility of seeing Peter that very evening. It would be the first time she laid eyes on him in the past two years. She was ashamed to admit it, even to herself, but she'd taken great pains in getting ready. She'd changed dresses twice, settling on the deep green cape dress that brought out the shine in her brown eyes. And she redone her hair three times before she'd been satisfied with the way it looked beneath her *kapp*.

She'd even bemoaned the lack of a bigger mirror to observe herself in, which she knew was downright shameful. If she wasn't careful, her vanity would get the best of her and the Lord God would not be pleased at all.

"Your cheeks are all red," Lizzie told her. "You sick or something?"

Sadie blanched. Was her excitement so obvious? And did it make her look sick? She was ready to dash into the bathroom to check herself yet once again in the small mirror hanging over the sink, but her mother interrupted.

"She looks fine," insisted her mother. "Mind your tongue, Lizzie."

When Sadie and her brothers were finally in the pony cart to leave, Sadie took a deep breath and forced herself to relax. She was getting herself all worked up for nothing. Chances were, Peter wouldn't be there anyway. Her mother didn't know everything.

Sadie would be better served to put her mind on Aaron. She'd received another letter from him just that afternoon. His words ran through her mind as the cart got underway.

Dear Sadie,

Thank you for your letter. I was right glad to receive it. Sounds like you'll be busy there. Things have slowed down for the winter and at times, I find that I don't have enough to keep me busy. Of course, Mamm is baking every minute of the day, and then storing the goods for Christmas. We'll be hosting her family and my dat's this year, so a lot of food is called for.

After Sadie had read the first paragraph earlier, she'd found herself relaxing. It was just a newsy sort of note, nothing too personal. But then, she'd continued and realized she'd been premature in her judgement.

I find myself frustrated with you so far away. As you know, our courtship hadn't gotten too far before you left.

Courtship? They'd gone riding a few times, but she hadn't truly considered it a courtship yet. She'd hoped he was serious about her, as she yearned to have a family of her own. But when she first read his words, she cringed, as if she didn't want his attention. Which didn't really make sense. Aaron was a fine catch and would make a fine beau.

If you do return at Christmas, can you get word to me? If the snow isn't too bad, I want to take you for a ride right away. I'd also like to take you to dinner in Ainesburg. There's a real good café that serves delicious food. Maybe you know it? The Wheel? It's run by Mennonites, and I think you'll like it.

Write soon, Sadie. I miss you. I hope you and your family are all well.

Your beau,

Aaron

Sadie had read his closing over and over and over, her eyes stuck on the word *beau*. Strange how quickly he'd made that leap. He must be feeling mighty confident. She didn't mind his confidence, but she wasn't completely sure it was right for her to consider him her beau. Not when she was fighting feelings for Peter.

She hadn't led Aaron on, had she? Even as the pony cart rolled down the road, she didn't think so. She'd never said anything to give Aaron false ideas.

"You're sure quiet," Roger said to her. "You okay?"

Sadie blinked. "Of course, I'm okay." Her breath trailed out in white wisps, disappearing into the frigid air.

"I'm gonna make sure I go in one of them vans tonight," Mark said.

Roger made a face at him. "You usually aren't so puny in the cold. What aren't you saying?"

Mark's face turned an immediate deep red. "Nothin'. And it is cold. Real cold."

Roger's eyes narrowed. "*Ach,* I know the reason."

"It ain't nothin'," Mark said quickly.

"It's that Mennonite girl. The one with the pretty blond hair. You like her," Roger claimed. "*Mamm* and *Dat* will have a fit."

"I don't like no one." Mark's shoulders rose close to his ears. "Quit telling tales."

Roger laughed. "Now it all makes sense. You're hoping that girl comes with her *dat* to drive us, and you want to ride in the same van as her."

"I do not!"

But it was clear to Sadie that he most certainly did. Sweet on a Mennonite girl? Roger was right—*Mamm* and *Dat* would have a fit. Of course, Mark was only thirteen, so no real concern was needed. Right? But hadn't she fallen for Peter when she was hardly older than that.

"I won't tattle," Roger was saying. He craned his neck, looking at Sadie who was sitting behind them. "You won't tell, will you?"

She made a show of pressing her lips together, and then she laughed. "Course not. I can keep a secret."

"You're both crazy," Mark grumbled, looking out over the empty fields.

By the time they reached the Fishers, Sadie's stomach was grinding with nerves. She wasn't even sure she wanted to get out of the cart. She glanced around at the array of buggies and carts, as if they would tell her whether Peter was there or not. Her brothers probably could decipher whose cart was whose, but she wasn't about to ask.

Roger pulled up on the reins and then jumped down to unhitch Bessie. Mark didn't even make a pretense of helping. He was stretching his neck every which way, clearly checking out the three vans that were parked near the porch. Sadie needed to get out. She could hardly spend the evening perched on the old apple crate they used for an extra seat in the pony cart.

She climbed out and stood next to Mark. He gave her a look. "Well, go on in," he said. "I'll come in with Roger."

She nodded and made her way past the barn toward the Fisher house. Smatterings of youth here and there all hurried inside, as there was no reason to dally in the cold. Sadie took a steadying breath and climbed the porch steps. She didn't know whether to pray that Peter would be there or not. Inwardly, she scoffed. As if she could pray such a selfish prayer anyway.

Chapter Seven

Peter leaned against the far wall of the front room, watching the youth as they assembled. There was a buzz of excitement in the air, and the chatter was animated and quite loud. Josh and James Yoder had just cracked up laughing at some private joke, and he noted that more than a few of the girls were gazing at the twins longingly.

He wished he felt the same carefree anticipation for the evening. But all he truly felt was a rock in his stomach as he wondered whether Sadie would show up. And then he felt guilt press on his shoulders. He shouldn't be excited to see an old girlfriend, not when his wife of less than a year hadn't lived to see anyone. He gulped in a breath. He couldn't think like that. He'd done enough thinking like that, and all it gave him was a raging headache and a punch to his heart.

He shouldn't have let his mother talk him into coming. He knew she meant well, but she had no idea how he felt in these public situations. He should have stayed home in his *daadi haus* and read the *Farmer's Almanac*. He grimaced.

He was sad, sad, sad.

He glanced toward the door and froze. There she was. She *had come*. His breath twisted in his throat, cutting off all air. Instant sweat covered his body, even though the room wasn't overly warm. He stood up straight, shifting his weight from one foot to the other. Would she see him? Would she acknowledge him?

He tried to swallow. He rubbed his hands on his thighs.

And then she glanced his way, and he saw the shock on her face. Their eyes locked for a fraction of a second and then she looked away. He gulped. She was beautiful, just like before. Her face was elfin-looking, sweet, youthful, and there was something magnetic about her. The way she carried herself, the way she stood, the way she looked at people as if she were really deeply seeing them.

He wanted her to look his way again. He wanted to see the light in her brown eyes, wanted to know what she was thinking. She'd appeared stunned to see him. Hadn't she been expecting to see him? A horrifying thought jerked through him. Maybe she hadn't been thinking of him at all. Maybe she hadn't thought of him since she'd left Hollybrook so many months before.

He huffed his breath out as disappointment raged through him. But what had he thought? That she'd see him and run right over, telling him how wonderful he was and how she'd missed him dearly? *Ach*, but he was a fool. He'd married someone else. Why would she possibly be thinking of him?

She was greeting some of the girls, and they were all chatting excitedly. They were clearly glad to see her again. Just like he was. He couldn't pull his eyes away, and she must have felt it. For a second, her gaze flittered his way, and when she saw him looking at her, she quickly averted her eyes, focusing again on her friends.

He blinked hard and gave himself a shake. He couldn't be seen staring at her. He couldn't be seen mooning over her. He couldn't abide being teased or scrutinized. What was the matter with him? He wanted to leave. But how would that look? Well, he shouldn't care how it would look. And in a large part, he didn't care. But if he left, he would hear about it from his mother, and he didn't know if he had enough energy to fight that storm. Sighing heavily, he forced himself to move—forced himself to go over to the twins and start talking.

Sadie clamped her eyes on Marcy, willing herself to hear what her friend was saying. But all she could really hear was the pounding of her heart in her ears. She felt faint, as if she could fall over any minute. Which, of course, she couldn't. How would she explain that?

Oh, I'm sorry for fainting—it's just that I saw my former beau and I'm still in love with him.

The roar in her ears became deafening. Was it true? Was she still in love with him? Her pulse increased, and she felt bile rise in her throat. She couldn't love him. He'd chosen someone else, and she couldn't bear going back to that agony.

Aaron. Aaron. Aaron. He liked her. Maybe even loved her. *Aaron. Aaron. Aaron.* Yes, think on him. Safer. Much safer.

Someone was clapping. Sadie gave a jolt and looked to where Benjamin Fisher stood. He grinned at everyone as the chatter died down.

"We're going to divide up into teams. We've already decided whose to be in charge of each team. They'll tell you which Christmas carols you're singing. We've got three vans hired to take some of you a bit further into town. One of the groups is going to Hollybrook's nursing home. You'll stay there the entire time. Last year, those folks loved us coming, and we hope to go every year from now on. The rest of you, just follow the schedule that your leader has."

He stopped and rubbed his hands together.

"Now, I ain't against you choosing who you want to be with. But we don't want to take forever to get underway. Don't forget that the missus has prepared a good number of treats for you when you return. We want you all back by eight-thirty or so. Now, if the four leaders will stand up here, the rest of you just go to one of them and we'll be on our way."

There was a scuffle as everyone divided themselves into groups. Sadie wished she was back home. She shouldn't have come. But then, was it right to allow her reaction to Peter to have so much control over her? She squared her shoulders and swallowed down her nausea.

"Come with us," Marcy said, pulling her sleeve.

She stumbled after Marcy into the group led by Jed Sutter. She purposefully didn't look to see where Peter ended up. Better that she completely ignore him.

"Sadie."

She froze, every muscle turning hard with dread. Slowly, she turned around and there he stood. So close that she could reach out and touch him. Someone bumped him while rushing to one of the groups and he momentarily lost his balance, tipping even closer to her. She sucked in her breath, and her eyes stretched wide. A panicked look covered his face as he regained his balance and stepped back.

"All right team," Jed said. "We're the walkers tonight."

Sadie gladly turned to give Jed her full attention. She was surprised that her intense staring didn't bore holes in the poor guy.

"Everyone bundled up? We're heading first to Old Mae's place. She loves it when we come. Let's head out."

All the groups were moving outside. There were lots of excited giggles and talking as three groups piled into the waiting vans. Sadie wondered why they were taking vans in the first place? Why not go by buggy or wagon? Although, she supposed it was safer to go by van in the dark. Especially if they were going all the way into town. Sadie had half a notion to defect from her group and climb into a van herself, but Marcy had a grip on her arm.

"I love caroling, don't you?" she said. "And Jed's a *gut* singer. This is going to be so fun."

Sadie put on a smile and nodded. "*Jah.* I'm looking forward to it."

"You have such a pretty voice," Marcy went on. "I remember that from before. You know, before you left for Ohio."

Sadie could barely concentrate on Marcy's words. Had Marcy just complimented her? That was unusual to be sure. She needed to respond. "Um. Thank you, Marcy," she uttered, now trying to sneak a look behind her. Maybe Peter would go with one of the groups in the vans.

Jed made a huge circular motion with his arm for everyone to follow him. "Might as well sing along the way," he said, his breath puffing out in clouds of white. "Let's start with *O Little Town of Bethlehem*."

He got them started and their voices rose in a full, rich sound as they made their way out to the road. Sadie joined in, still wondering if Peter was behind her somewhere. She found herself trying to squelch rising excitement at the thought of him so close. *Ach.* What was the matter with her? Her emotions were a jumbled broil of confusion.

Marcy was happily singing with gusto, moving up closer to the front of the group. Sadie didn't follow, staying where she was in the middle of the group. Jed switched them to *Away in the Manger*, and Sadie smiled. This was her favorite Christmas hymn. She loved visualizing the baby Jesus in the hay, surrounded by such love.

"Sadie."

And there he was again. She faltered only slightly before turning to look at him. She carefully smiled.

"Hello, Peter." They both slowed their walk.

They were jostled as some of the youth surged around them, straining toward the front.

"I didn't know you were returning," Peter said, and he was easily heard as the singers moved forward. "You here to stay?"

His voice. How her heart used to tremble at the sound. How she used to become excited whenever she heard him, latching onto his words, wondering if he was about to come over and speak with her.

"I-I don't know," she stammered. She sucked in a long breath. "I left *Mammi* alone for Christmas, which I didn't like to do. So, I might be going back."

Occasional street lamps shed light on the dark road. Some of the youth carried lanterns which helped light their way, so there was enough light for Sadie to easily see Peter's expression. His gaze was intent on hers, and she felt like she was perched on a display shelf.

"Your family must be right glad to have you home."

"*Jah*," she said. She increased her speed; they were being left behind.

He touched her arm, stopping her. She glanced down at his hand, feeling his touch race through her coat and settle on her skin. She blinked. His fingers were long and strong, and she imagined he had calluses on his palm where it rested on her sleeve.

"I'm sorry," he said, his voice jerking out unceremoniously.

She gasped. What was he doing? She glanced around quickly. Was anyone overhearing? The singing continued, and she didn't think anyone was paying them any mind. But still, she was uncomfortable. In truth, she wanted to talk to him. But there? And now?

She swallowed and continued walking. His hand dropped from her sleeve.

"Sadie?"

She stopped while the others continued down the road. Maybe she wanted to talk to him more than she'd thought. She looked up at him and waited.

"Before. Before you left Hollybrook. I ... well, I didn't treat you kindly." His voice softened, and she braced herself against the feelings of affection that caught hold of her. "I've regretted that for a long time. I'm sorry. You deserved better."

She tilted her head and frowned slightly. What an odd way to phrase it. She deserved better? She supposed she did; although, she'd never thought of it in such terms. All she knew was that her heart had been broken. And now here she was, standing before the very person who had broken it.

He looked at her expectantly, waiting for some response.

"It was a long time ago," she murmured.

"*Jah,* it was. But still, I've felt bad about it all this time."

Had he? Something in her stirred. Something warm and tender.

"Will you forgive me, Sadie?"

"I-I..." Her throat tightened, and she felt tears burning in the back of her eyes. She swallowed. "*Jah.* Of course."

She was going to cry. She felt it, and she couldn't—absolutely *couldn't*—let him see it. He'd think she was crazy to be crying over something that happened so long ago. Without another word, she turned away from him and hurried to catch up with the others. The tears were coming now, and she wiped at them furiously before joining the end of the line.

The words to *Good King Wenceslas* rang about her. She opened her mouth to join in, but her voice wouldn't come. He had apologized. He had felt badly. He'd recognized that he'd been heartless toward her. She wanted to sob out loud all over again, and she couldn't understand why. She'd done her crying months ago. Why would she want to weep it out again?

Was she hoping to start something new with him? Was that it? She couldn't. She just couldn't. Besides, him apologizing meant nothing. He was only trying to ease his guilt.

She put her arms around her waist and leaned into the cold, hugging herself—attempting to calm herself. But the tears continued to come. They were walking a stretch of road between streetlights, and no one at the back of the line was carrying a lantern.

She'd never been so grateful for the dark.

Chapter Eight

Peter stood still, watching Sadie dart away from him. Not just walk away, mind you. But run. She'd caught up with the group now and didn't turn around. He sighed heavily, his breath gushing out in complete frustration. He'd thought apologizing was the thing to do. He'd thought she'd forgive him and maybe they could be friends again.

He ran his hand over his beard, annoyed at his own stupidity.

She said she forgave him, and maybe she had. But she certainly didn't like him. And she was the only one in the entire district that he wanted to be with right then—which was alarming to say the least. Oh, he had a lot of friends. And family, too. But it was Sadie who drew him. It was her gentle smile he wanted to see; her happy laughter he wanted to hear.

Clearly, she didn't want a thing to do with him. He'd messed it up but good. Strains from the Christmas hymns filtered back to him and a sudden stab of loneliness pierced his heart. He realized at that moment that he'd been eagerly anticipating this evening. Eagerly anticipating the moment when he'd see her again. But he'd imagined a much different result.

His shoulders sank as he continued to stand there like a lost puppy in a storm. He knew he should probably catch up with the group, but he couldn't do it. He simply couldn't do it. He was in no condition to be with a bunch of people that evening. He wasn't even fit company for himself. Sighing again, he turned back toward the Fisher place. He'd hitch up his buggy and go home. He could tell his mother that he'd attended. He didn't have to mention how long he had stayed. Plus, no one would miss him.

Least of all Sadie.

Old Mae opened her door and pushed through the screen to stand on her large wrap-around porch. She was huddled inside a shawl, grinning with joy. "*Ach!* You came to carol for an old woman. Now, this is quite a sight."

"Do you have a favorite Christmas hymn?" Jed asked.

Her eyes twinkled in the lantern light. "I like them all, young man. You sing whatever you wish."

Jed led them in *Angels We Have Heard on High* and the group sang with fervor. When the *Glorias* began, Marcy pushed her way back to Sadie.

"I want to hear you sing," she said close to Sadie's ear.

Sadie did her best not to disappoint, but her voice was hardly at its best. It warbled and she only just kept herself from bursting into tears again. She glanced around but didn't see Peter anywhere. Had he left? Or was he walking so slowly that he'd catch up with them eventually? And why was her mind glued to thoughts of him? Before singing out another *gloria*, she inhaled deeply, feeling the bitter cold sink into her lungs.

Marcy grinned and nudged her and added her voice to the mix. When they finished, Old Mae clapped with delight.

"Would you all like some hot tea?" she asked.

"Thank you, but *nee*," Jed said. "We have a lot of territory to cover before eight-thirty. But we'll sing a few more songs before we go."

Sadie's voice improved as they continued. Peter hadn't shown up yet, and she decided to not care whether he did or not. She began to enjoy herself. Marcy was good company, chattering between songs. It had grown colder, though, and her feet and hands began to go numb. She rubbed her mittens together as they moved to other farms, mainly singing to the elders.

After four more farms and a good couple of miles, Jed turned them about to head back. By the time they'd all trudged through the icy air back to the Fishers, all Sadie could think about once again was Peter. As they sat around and sipped hot chocolate and indulged in a vast array of homemade cookies and Christmas candy, a loneliness crept over Sadie—which was absurd considering she was in the midst of a group of talking, laughing, excited youth.

But still, the loneliness hovered. She was ready to go home far before her brothers wanted to leave, and so she had to stay, engaging in the frivolity so no one would suspect her real feelings. She was exhausted when she finally settled into the cart, and her cheeks hurt from smiling. She pulled on her outer bonnet, tugging it over her ears. It was downright freezing out now, and the ride home was going to be uncomfortable to say the least.

Her brothers were full of happy talk about the caroling—even though the cute blond Mennonite daughter hadn't been there, and Sadie was relieved to sit quietly and just let them go at it. They didn't even notice her silence; they were still laughing and joshing as they pulled the cart into their drive. Roger yanked up on the reins, and they stopped in front of the barn.

"I'll help you unhitch," Mark offered, bolting out of the cart.

"Thank you for the ride," Sadie said and climbed out. "I'm going in. See you in the morning."

"*Jah*, sure," Roger called over his shoulder. They were already seeing to Bessie.

Sadie hurried into the house and shed her outer clothing. It was dark. Everyone had already turned in. She felt about on the dining table, locating the lantern and matches. She lit the wick and went upstairs, careful to avoid stepping on the creaky third and eighth steps. No need to wake anyone.

Inside her room, she set the lantern on her dresser. She quickly changed into her nightgown and then she went to her bedside stand and removed the tablet and pen. She was foolish to think that anything could happen between her and Peter. She wasn't even sure she wanted it to. There was simply too much emotion involved. Too much past. Too much pain.

And he was likely still grieving his wife. His *wife.* She'd thought that *she* would be his wife. She shivered. She didn't want to go there anymore. Not in her mind or her heart. It was too hard. There was too much... *what?* She didn't know. All she knew was that her emotions were a painful jumble.

She looked down at the tablet in her hand. She gripped the pen more tightly and perched on the edge of her bed. There was none of this confusion with Aaron. None. It was straightforward and simple. He liked her and wanted to court her. She liked him well enough, didn't she?

With Aaron, there was no tumultuous past. There was no memory of searing pain. There was nothing to apologize for or to forgive. Simple. She opened her notebook and began to write.

. . .

Dear Aaron,

The youth went caroling tonight. It was mighty cold, but I think we brought some Christmas cheer to folks. We were in four groups. Three groups went in hired vans, but I was with the walkers. My friend Marcy and I stuck together all evening.

Afterward, we had hot chocolate and all sorts of goodies. I think Tamera Fisher must have baked for days in preparation. And she's a gut cook, so I'm sure you can guess how delicious it all was.

I hope everything is going well with you. It's not long now till Christmas Day. I might talk with my parents tomorrow about going back to Ainesburg to be with Mammi. I'm more eager than ever to get back to Ohio.

To leave Peter, you mean. Sadie swallowed and stared at her letter, unsure how to sign it. Last time in his letter, Aaron had called himself her beau, but she couldn't bring herself to write such an intimate closing. She finally settled with, *Your friend, Sadie.*

She folded it up and placed it on top of her bedside stand. She'd address the envelope and send the letter the next day. She stared at the wall, watching the subtle dance of light as the lantern flickered. She'd done the right thing by writing Aaron.

She pulled back her quilt and settled into bed, reaching over and lowering the wick until the lantern snuffed out. She pulled the covers up to her chin, trying to get warm. The upstairs was always cold; maybe she needed to put another quilt on her bed. She lay on her side and drew her knees up to her chest.

She thought about Aaron and how nice he was, how handsome he was, too. With determination, she kept her mind on him and on the times they'd been together. On their conversations. On their laughter.

But when she fell asleep, her thoughts had wandered right back to Peter.

Chapter Nine

Sadie insisted that her mother rest all the next morning. She put up a fuss, but Sadie didn't relent. She enlisted both Matilda and Lizzie in a massive clean-up. They not only did the normal housework, they dug deep, waxing floors, dusting the occasional cobweb from the ceiling, even re-organizing the basement. By the noon meal, both her sisters were complaining.

"Look here," Sadie said, "a new *boppli* is coming, so we have to have this house in perfect condition. Besides, you won't always have me to help, so best to get this done now."

"What? You're leaving again?" Matilda asked, her brow scrunching into a frown. "I thought you were back to stay."

"I get my room back," Lizzie said, and then had the decency to look guilty.

"I don't know how long I'll be here," Sadie said. "But I need you to be *gut* and helpful to *Mamm* all the time. You hear me?"

"We're always helpful," Matilda said. "Go and ask her."

"I didn't mean you weren't," Sadie said, pulling the knot of her sister's bandana. "I just want you to be even more helpful."

"You think it's gonna be a girl?" Lizzie asked.

"Could be."

"I hope it is. We don't need no more boys around here."

Sadie laughed. "All right. I need someone to boil the eggs. We're going to have potato salad with our roast."

"Potato salad in winter?" Matilda asked. "Yum."

The three of them laughed and got right at the cooking.

Sadie waited until her dad was in the front room with her mother before approaching them. She realized that she likely couldn't go to *Mammi's* for Christmas. Her mother was going to need more and more help as time progressed. Probably, after the baby came, her younger sisters could take over as *Mamm* would be up and about more easily.

But still, Sadie's heart was heavy over leaving her grandmother. She also wanted to see Aaron again. She wanted to know how she would feel when she was with him. Was love growing on her part? It was hard to know while she was there in Hollybrook. Peter muddied the waters for her, and she was anxious to get away. At least for a little bit.

"*Mamm*? *Dat*? May I talk to you?" she asked, sticking her head into the front room.

"Of course, child. Come in." *Mamm* took her feet off the cushions and made to sit up.

"*Nee, Mamm*. Stay where you are. I'll sit in a rocker." Sadie pulled a rocker over closer to the davenport and the easy chair where her dad was sitting.

"What is it?" *Dat* asked.

"I'm worried about *Mammi*."

Dat leaned forward. "What is it? Is she failing?"

Sadie shook her head. "*Nee. Nee.* It's just that she'll be alone for Christmas and it makes me sad."

"Didn't you offer to bring her here?" *Mamm* asked.

"*Jah*, but she won't come." Sadie touched her chin. "You know, I always thought it was just plain stubbornness, but I think it's more."

"What do you mean?" *Mamm* asked.

"I think she's afraid the trip will be too hard on her. She's not failing, *Dat*. At least, I don't think so. But she's not real strong, either."

Dat got abruptly up and started to pace. "We must get her here. That's all there is to it."

Mamm held up her hand. "You want to go back, don't you? You don't want to be here."

Sadie's cheeks went hot. "*Nee.* I'm happy to be here. I'm happy to help."

Mamm shook her head. "You want to go back." She sighed. "Now don't give me that guilty look. I understand. I'm not faulting you, child."

"Well, I am," *Dat* interjected, his voice sharp. "Your *mamm* needs you, Sadie."

"I know," Sadie said. "And I told you I'm happy to be here."

He scowled and gave her a dubious look.

"Arguing won't solve a thing," *Mamm* said. "You need to go back. At least for Christmas Day."

"And pay a van for a one-day stay?" asked Dat. "That seems mighty frivolous."

"It's important to Sadie. And I don't like the idea of your *mamm* being alone for Christmas, either." *Mamm* smoothed her dress over her legs. "We'll be fine for a few days. Why don't you stay for three to four days, Sadie? I'll be fine for that amount of time. Besides, there will be others around on the holidays who can help."

"Like who?" *Dat* asked. "Your sister? She's got such a houseful of *kinner*, she don't know which way is up."

Mamm chuckled. "Dan, you're terrible."

"It's true."

"Maybe so. But still, I'll be fine. Sadie, you go ahead and make arrangements."

"But we want you directly back here. Three days, not four. Understood?" *Dat* asked.

Sadie stood, hardly believing how the conversation had gone. "*Jah,* I understand. Thank you. And you're sure, *Mamm*?"

"I'm sure." Her mother gave her a warm smile. "Now, would you kindly go to the Feed & Supply for me? I'm thinking about making some cinnamon rolls, and we're mighty short on cinnamon. Plus, we need to make some sugar cookies to decorate for Christmas. I'm needing more lard."

"You don't need to be baking..." *Dat* started.

"Lands sake," *Mamm* cried. "I'm not on my deathbed here. I still have some vinegar left in me."

Dat grinned. "That you do, Bonnie. That you do."

Sadie left them as they continued to tease one another. After all these years, the fondness and love between her parents was still a tangible thing. She sighed, wishing she could have that with someone. Peter again flashed through her mind. Disgusted, she quickened her pace.

She refocused on Aaron. Was he the one?

She went upstairs to fetch her thicker socks. When she passed her sisters' room, they were both in there flounced on the bed, reading. "Either of you want to go to the Feed & Supply with me?" she asked.

"*Nee*," they both chorused at once.

"It's too cold," Lizzie added. "Besides, I'm at the best part of this book."

"How many times have you read that?" Matilda asked. "About a hundred?"

Sadie grinned. "It's not very warm up here, you two. Why don't you both go downstairs to read?"

"We like it up here," Matilda said.

Lizzie grunted and turned a page.

Sadie left them, took her socks from her drawer and put them on over her thinner pair, and then she went downstairs to bundle up for her errand.

Chapter Ten

Funny how a person got used to the cold. When the first frost hit in fall, it was always a shock to the system, but by mid-December, Sadie supposed they'd all toughened up. She had to admit that she did like the aura of frozen stillness on cold days. That afternoon, she felt like she was the only one in the world. No one passed her on the road, not even a motor car. The clip clop of Bessie's hooves echoed around her in the crisp air. She took a long deep breath, enjoying the barren countryside.

She did love it there in Hollybrook. It surprised her how content she felt at that moment to be there, riding peacefully to the Feed & Supply. If only *Mammi* would agree to move. But if she did, Sadie wouldn't be going back to Ohio. She wouldn't be seeing Aaron again. And if things between her and Aaron went well, she would be moving back to Ainesburg permanently.

Well, that was what she wanted, wasn't it?

A crow cawed from a nearby tree and then took flight, swooping overhead—a black shadow against the stark blue sky. The sound reminded her of summer days in the field and all of the family working together to ensure a good harvest.

Bessie snorted, and Sadie clicked her tongue. "You're doing fine, girl," she called out. "We're almost there."

A few minutes later, she was pulling into the large parking area at the Feed & Supply. She imagined Eliza Troyer inside, fussing over her inventory, watching the customers, sticking her nose into everyone's business. Some things never changed.

She glanced around the lot. Looked to be only two other customers there. She sighed, knowing she was in for the grand inquisition from Eliza. She tugged Bessie to a stop and looped the reins over the post at the side of the cart. She got out, feeling a bit stiff after the cold ride. She was patting Bessie's neck when she heard his voice.

"Sadie?"

She tensed. Of all things, why did *he* have to be there? Why did he have to be one of the two only other customers right then?

She turned and smiled at him. "Hello, Peter."

He broke into a wide grin and his expression turned animated. It occurred to her that he was truly glad to see her, which immediately made her both pleased and wary.

"Out running errands, I see," he said.

"*Jah.* And you, too, by the looks of it."

He chuckled, holding up his paper bag. "Picking up a few things for Jess."

Jess…? Oh, right. Jess Gundy, his father-in-law. "I see," she said.

"About the other night—"

She interrupted him. "I'm right sorry about the way I ran off so quick-like. Can't imagine what got into my head. I wanted to thank you for apologizing."

"I meant it," he said, stepping closer. He was so tall. Stretched above her like that, she felt small and dainty and a bit overcome. Her breathing went shallow. His dark blue eyes softened until it was as if they were caressing her without a touch. Everything inside her tingled, and she felt her chest tighten with yearning.

She had no idea what to say. Why did he still have such power over her? She didn't want to subject herself to him again. She couldn't. It could only be worse now. She didn't want to deal with his grief over another woman.

She moved back. "I'm going to Ohio for Christmas."

He blanched. “What?”

“I’m going back.”

He blinked, and she saw his confusion. His expression clouded. “You’ve only just arrived.”

“I know, but *Mammi* is alone. And there are others I need to see...” She left the phrase hanging. Shame flashed through her. Why had she said that? One didn’t discuss courting with others—*particularly* old beaus. What was she trying to do?

“Others?”

She raised her chin. She’d started it... “*Jah*. Others.”

“By others, you mean a beau.” His words were clipped and something fell over his eyes. Something invisible, but there just the same.

“Perhaps.”

He stared at her, and the silence between them deepened and stretched and yawned as if a crevice was splitting open between them—growing wider and wider. He blinked again, and a muscle beside his jaw twitched.

“So, you’re courting.”

She bit her bottom lip. So. He was going to be outright with it. She didn’t remember him as flouting convention so boldly before. He’d changed, and despite her misgivings, she found herself strangely intrigued.

His eyes probed hers, and she knew he was waiting for a response, but for some reason, she didn't want to give him one. Her lips parted slightly, and she remained silent.

"We used to be friends, Sadie," he said finally, his voice edged with sadness.

His sadness crept into her, inching into her throat, her chest, and down her arms until all she felt was his heaviness. His pain. She struggled to draw in a breath. This wasn't fair. Wasn't right. She shouldn't be standing with him there, squarely in public, discussing beaus and courtship and apologies.

She tried to swallow, but in the frigid air, her throat ached with dryness.

"Are you happy?" he asked abruptly, startling her.

"Happy?"

"*Jah*. Are you happy?"

What a ridiculous question. Was she happy? That wasn't the aim of life. Life was about pleasing God, following the *Ordnung*, serving her family and her fellow district members. Her own happiness was not paramount to anything. Why was he asking such a question?

He took another step closer and if she tried, she could feel his breath on her cheeks as he studied her face. "You always were so beautiful."

She gasped and nearly lost her balance. "I-I need to go," she said. "*Mamm* is expecting her supplies."

She darted away from him, darted away from his gaze, his presence, his power over her. Her eyes misted over so that she could barely see the store's steps in front of her. She grabbed the railing and hurried up the steps and inside the door. The bell above the door tinkled. She was inside; she should feel safe now.

But safety was not what she felt. Instead, all she felt was total confusion and desperation. No. No. That wasn't right.

Mired and twisted amidst it all, indeed overpowering it all, was love.

And then all she felt was fear.

She couldn't do this. She couldn't go back to such fervent love for Peter. Her tears spilled over, and she wiped at them frantically.

"Why, if it ain't Sadie Verkler," came a shrill voice from behind the counter.

Sadie plastered a smile on her face, blinking her tears away. "Hello, Eliza," she said. "How are you?"

"Fair to middling." The woman's piercing eyes took her in. "You all right?"

Sadie widened her smile until she felt her cheeks nearly split.

"Of course. I'm fine. Maybe you can point me toward the cinnamon and the lard."

Sadie knew full well where the spices were and where the lard was, but anything to distract the district's busybody. Her ploy worked, as Eliza Troyer strode out from behind the counter and led her to the second aisle. "You'll find them here, child. I'm a bit surprised that you forgot. How long have you been gone now?"

"A couple of years," Sadie said, studying the rows of spices as if they were jewels.

"How's that *grossmammi* of yours? When's she coming over this way?" Eliza's voice was like a stinging insect, sharp and insistent.

"*Ach*, we've tried to get her here. She won't budge." Sadie nearly wept with relief to be talking about her grandmother. Her eyes were good and dry now, so she could face Eliza when she spoke.

"How many pounds of lard do you need?"

Sadie pointed to the smallest can. "That should do it."

Eliza bent down and scooped it up, groaning slightly. "What else are you needing?"

"*Nee*, this is all," Sadie said.

They moved to the counter again, and Sadie made her transaction. She took her purchases and left the store.

Outside, she glanced around nervously, thinking Peter might still be around, but she didn't see him. She walked back to her cart and set the brown sack into the bed. Just as she was ready to climb up into the cart, she sucked in her breath. There on the wooden seat lay a shiny black stone, shaped like a star. Sadie recognized it immediately.

It was the stone Peter had carried around with him for years. He'd found it at Edmund's Pond when he was a boy. He'd been intrigued by its shape, certain that it was a star fallen from the heavens. Of course, when he grew older, he realized that it was no such thing. But still, he kept it. He told Sadie that having it with him brought back the fun, carefree days of his childhood. Sadie had always thought he was being quite fanciful, but Peter was like that. He enjoyed small things and things he thought unique.

Her hand trembled as she picked up the stone from the seat. She brought it to her face and felt its cold smoothness on her cheek. She lowered it quickly. Why had he left it there? Was he giving it to her? And if so, why?

She slipped it inside her mitten where it fell against her palm. She left it there the entire way home.

Chapter Eleven

Matilda dashed through the side door in a whirl of cold and fluttering snowflakes. "Sadie!" she hollered and then stopped short, nearly running into Sadie as she was sweeping the wash room. "*Ach,* you're here," Matilda said. She thrust an envelope at her. "You got a letter."

Sadie's brow rose. Had *Mammi* written? She hoped so. "Thank you," she told her sister, taking the envelope and looking at the handwriting on the envelope. There was no return address and this was not her *mammi's* script. Nor was it Aaron's.

"Who's it from?" Matilda asked.

"Don't rightly know," Sadie answered, setting the broom aside.

"Well, open it."

Sadie gave her sister a look. "I'll be in my room," she said, turning to leave.

"Ain't you going to open it here?"

Sadie smiled. "*Nee,* I'm not going to open it here. Why don't you finish up the sweeping?"

Matilda groaned and made a face. "Do I got to?"

"*Jah*, you have to. Now, get on it, dear little sister." She picked the broom back up and pushed the handle toward Matilda.

Matilda reluctantly took it. "But you'll tell me who it's from, right? Is it *Mammi*?"

"*Nee*, it's not *Mammi*. Now, get to sweeping."

Sadie wasn't sure who the letter was from. She'd hoped to hear from *Mammi* as she'd already let her know she was coming for Christmas. The only other person who would write her would be Aaron, and since she'd had a letter from his yesterday, it wasn't him. And she already knew it wasn't his handwriting, anyway.

She hurried through the dining area and climbed the stairs two at a time—once she was sure her mother wasn't watching her. She scurried to her bedroom and shut the door, going to her bed and sinking onto the heavy layers of quilts. She ripped the envelope open and took out the letter, unfolding it carefully. By now, she had a niggling suspicion who the letter was from and when she saw the signature, she gasped.

. . .

Dear Sadie,

I would like to see you. I figure this letter should get to you Saturday afternoon, so I will be waiting at the end of your drive Saturday evening at seven-thirty. I have no idea whether you'll come or not, but I'm asking you to please come.

If you don't show up, I won't bother you again.

Peter

Sadie gaped at his words. He was coming that evening? And for what? He'd already apologized, so there was really nothing left to say. Her hand went to her waistband, where she had hidden his stone. She'd turned the fabric up to form a sort of pocket, where the stone fit snugly. Why she was keeping it there she had no real idea; it had just seemed like the best place for it.

She should have tossed it away, into the shallow snow out back by the garden. But she couldn't do that. She knew how much the stone meant to Peter. Well, she could give it back to him that evening.

She stood up and began pacing circles on her rag rug. No. She wasn't going to meet him. It could only lead to more confusion and more heartache. But why did he want to see her? Maybe he wanted his stone back; but then, why didn't he just say so? She glanced to the row of pegs by her bedroom door. Her purple gown was comely. She'd taken great pains when she'd made it some months ago. She'd been feeling a bit vain at the time, trying to make a dress that would make her look pretty. Peter might appreciate such a dress in such a color.

She stopped pacing. What in the world was she thinking?

It was in the thirties outside. If she went, he wouldn't even see her dress. She'd have to be bundled up to her chin to stay warm.

And she wasn't going to go out driving with him anyway. Why should she?

She resumed her pacing. Then she stopped and read his letter again. He didn't even give her time to respond by mail. Was he so sure of himself? She reread it a third time. No, he didn't sound sure. She glanced out the window into the upper naked branches of the huge oak tree in their front yard. She could see deserted nests where birds had diligently built them the summer before.

She let out her breath in a huge sigh. She wasn't going to go. She was going to ignore his summons and concentrate her thinking energy on her grandmother. And her mother. She stepped over to her bedside stand and opened the drawer, shoving the letter inside.

She needed to go down and check with her mother. Make

sure she didn't need anything. And then she could brew some tea and sit with her and chat about nothing in particular.

After that, supper would need to be prepared.

She was simply too busy to consider Peter's request. That was all there was to it.

Chapter Twelve

Peter dressed with care. He combed his hair and decided on his black felt hat instead of his straw one. He chose his black scarf and black gloves, too. He even washed his face before braving the cold to hitch up his buggy.

He hoped the Gundy's weren't around, watching through the window. He rarely if ever left with the buggy during the evening. In fact, the last time he'd gone out at night was to the Christmas caroling, and what a disaster that had been.

He strode quickly to the barn to get Champ. At least, Champ wouldn't mind the cold. That horse was ready to get out at every opportunity. Peter smiled. He often had to hold Champ back, keeping the reins taut, or the horse would go much too fast for comfort. When Peter first got the animal, he'd let Champ go, seeing just how fast he could take the buggy.

Too fast was the answer. Champ never seemed to forget that first ride, and he fussed and tossed his head, and even plowed the dirt with his front leg, forever wanting to do the same again.

Eloise had been afraid of Champ, preferring her parents' gentle old pony when she hitched up. So, Champ had become Peter's alone.

He took the horse from the stall, feeding him a handful of sugar cubes as he took him out into the night air. As expected, Champ nearly pranced with excitement.

"Whoa, there, boy," Peter said softly, close to his ear. "Settle down. You'll get to pull soon enough."

He slipped off his gloves, which made the hitching process much easier. Within fifteen minutes, he was in the buggy, gloves back on, ready to head to the Verkler farm. He was early. He'd be there well before seven-thirty.

No matter. He would wait.

Would Sadie show up? He truly didn't know. Nor did he know exactly what he was going to say. His emotions were a jumble that rested just below his throat, sometimes even clogging his breathing. He didn't have the patience to unravel it all. The only thing he knew for certain was that he wanted to see Sadie. Wanted to be with her. Wanted to watch her smile. Wanted to *make* her smile.

He must have been crazy to write that letter, to even be

attempting to see her. She wouldn't want to be with him. Hadn't she made that perfectly clear? And what had possessed him to put his stone in her pony cart? She might not have even seen it. It probably fell off the bench and was wedged into the corner of her cart somewhere.

She likely didn't remember that stone anyway. And in truth, he felt a bit naked without it. Stupid, he thought. He was acting like a downright idiot.

Well, it was too late now. If she did show, and he wasn't there, that would be the end of it, for sure and for certain. But he didn't want the end of it. Not anymore. He wanted a beginning. A new beginning. A fresh start where he could show Sadie how much she really meant to him.

He snapped the reins and Champ happily increased his speed, snorting his pleasure.

Peter should have warmed bricks to bring with him. He could have tucked them around Sadie's feet to keep her warm. Did he have time to go back? No. He wasn't that early.

His pulse increased and his breathing grew shallow. "Please be there, Sadie," he whispered. "Please be there."

Sadie finished washing the dishes and drained the sinks of the water. She squeezed out the washrag and hung it over the faucet to dry.

"We done?" Lizzie asked.

"*Jah*. We're done."

"Wanna play a game with us before *Dat* starts the Bible reading?"

Sadie glanced up at the clock. It was seven-fifteen. If she was going to meet Peter, she'd have to get a move on. But she wasn't going to meet Peter, was she?

"*Jah*. A game sounds nice."

Did the clock suddenly become louder? Sadie was certain the ticking sound was now hammering out the seconds as the hand moved around the clock. Seven-sixteen...

"Well, come on, then," Lizzie said, pulling on her arm. Sadie allowed herself to be dragged to the front room where Matilda had already set up the monopoly game on the coffee table.

"I'm red," she cried.

Sadie sat down on the floor on the other side of the coffee table. "I'll be yellow."

"Then, I'm gonna be blue."

Matilda set out the markers. "Ready?"

Sadie craned her head, trying to peer back into the kitchen to check the time. Of course, she couldn't see the clock from where she sat.

"I'll start," Lizzie declared.

"No fair. You started last time..." Matilda complained. "We'll let Sadie start."

Was it seven-seventeen or seven-eighteen by now? Was Peter already out there waiting for her? What did he want to say? Would she forever regret it if she didn't go out there to find out? And she still had his stone.

She should return it.

"Sadie?" Matilda said, giving her a light punch in the shoulder. "It's your turn."

Sadie licked her lips and swallowed. Her throat felt tight, and her heart was beating wildly now. She jumped up. "I can't play. I have to go."

"What?" Lizzie said.

"*Mamm,*" Sadie looked over to where her mother was resting on the davenport. "I'm going out for a bit."

Bonnie Verkler raised a brow but said nothing.

"Sorry, sisters." Sadie dashed out of the room and flew up the stairs. Even though Peter wouldn't see what dress she wore, she quickly slipped out of her everyday dress and her apron and put on the purple cape dress. She carefully enclosed Peter's stone in the waistband again. She patted her hair smooth under the *kapp* and nearly tripped going down the steps, she was in such a hurry.

She grabbed her heaviest cape from the wash room and twisted a scarf around her neck. She stepped into her black shoes, bending to tie them quickly. Then she put on her gloves and almost exploded out the side door. Her breath caught at the cold air as she dashed across the lawn.

It had to be past seven-thirty by now. He'd probably already come and gone. Irritated with herself, she increased her speed, racing now to the end of the drive. She reached the main road, panting heavily.

No buggy.

Tears burned her eyes. And then she heard it. A horse, clip-clopping away. There he was. He was leaving already.

Should she run after him? He wasn't going quickly at all. Yet. She could catch up to the buggy. But, land's sake, what would that look like? Her chasing after a buggy like a desperate girl? It would be downright humiliating is what.

"Peter!" she called loudly without thinking. But he'd never hear her. "Peter!"

She put her arms around herself, fighting tears. But the buggy had stopped. She sucked in her breath. The driver's door opened, and Peter stepped out. He stood beside the door, tall and lanky and incredibly beautiful.

In only a few long strides, he was beside her, looming over her, gazing down at her eyes, her nose, her lips.

"You came," he whispered.

"You left," she said, smiling now.

"I did. I figured you weren't coming. I should have waited longer."

She shrugged.

He cleared his throat. "Thank you for coming." His voice was husky. He took her gloved hand in his and led her back to the buggy.

Her heart pounded, and she could hear blood rushing in her ears. Even through her glove, she felt the energy of him zinging up her arm and into her chest. She tried to calm her breathing, but it was useless. She felt almost heady as she climbed into the buggy.

He hurried around to the other side and got in. He picked up the reins and smacked them on his horse's backside. "I'm sorry I don't have a better buggy with a heater," he said. "They've got some real nice ones these days."

"I'm fine," she said, folding her hands tightly in her lap as if holding on to herself for dear life.

"I thought we might just ride around the district if that suits."

"It suits," she replied. A sudden thought occurred to her. Was being there in Peter's buggy being unfaithful to Aaron? She squirmed in her seat. To Aaron's mind, it would be. She'd never outwardly agreed to them courting, but he assumed they were, and she hadn't said or done anything to disabuse him of the notion.

She shouldn't be there. It was wrong. She rustled under her cape and retrieved Peter's stone from her waistband. She held it out to him.

"Here is your stone."

She could see his face quite clearly in the yellow light of the lamps which were hung at both front corners of the buggy. She saw his frown and then the slight quiver at the corner of his lips. He stared at the stone as if he'd never seen it before. The mood in the buggy changed instantaneously. He shifted the reins to one hand and reached for the stone with his other.

"You don't want it?" he asked slowly, and his voice faltered.

Suddenly, she knew exactly what he'd been thinking when he'd left the stone for her. The truth of it shouted through her heart—her entire being. He wanted her back.

He *wanted her back*. She had no doubt of it.

The knowledge of it jolted inside her like a rush of roaring water. She watched him take the stone from her as if in slow motion. She watched his gloved fingers close around it and remove it from her hand. She watched him stare at the stone, and then she watched it disappear somewhere inside his coat. What had he done with it? He had no pockets.

But he was looking at her now, his eyes shadowed in the faint light. His expression was raw and she saw his yearning, his love, his sorrow. Her throat tightened, and she could barely draw a breath. She didn't know what to do.

She couldn't go back to him, could she? And what about Aaron? This was wrong. All wrong. But if it *was* wrong, why did she want to bury herself in Peter's arms? Why did she want to nestle into him and hear his heart beating against her ear? Why did she feel something ripping open inside of her?

"I'll take you back home," he said stiffly, now facing forward, every muscle of his face set. "This was a mistake."

She pressed her hand to her mouth, fighting tears. Longing raced through her. She wanted to speak, to say something, *anything*, but she couldn't. Nothing in her body seemed to be working properly. Nothing.

She remained stiff and upright and silent as he drove her straight back to her house. He stopped the buggy at the end of her drive. He remained still and didn't even look at her as she climbed out of his buggy and fled quickly across her yard.

Chapter Thirteen

Sadie cried herself to sleep that night. She cried for Peter. For herself. For Aaron. She even cried for Eloise. By the time sleep finally overcame her, her eyes were nearly swollen shut with crying. Somewhere in the middle of the night, she stirred, and everything came rushing back. She put her pillow over her head and tried to stop the thoughts, but it didn't help. All she could see was Peter's hard profile when she'd left him.

Was he sleeping that night? Or was he tossing and turning and thinking of her?

She groaned and flopped on her side, keeping her pillow over her head.

Sadie's bag was packed, and she was ready to go. Matilda stood by her side on the front porch, shivering.

"I wanted you to stay for Christmas," she whined.

Sadie took a deep breath. "I know you did, but *Mammi* is all by herself."

"She don't got to be." Matilda huffed out her breath.

"I'll try again, all right? I'll try to convince her to come to Hollybrook to live with us."

"Okay." Matilda thrust a piece of folded paper at her. "I drew a picture for her. Can you take it with you?"

Sadie smiled. "Of course, I can. She'll love it. Thank you, Matilda."

"And tell her I want to see her."

"I'll tell her that, too." Sadie gave Matilda a hug. "Now remember, I cooked ahead. I don't want *Mamm* in the kitchen much at all. You and Lizzie will see to it, won't you?"

"*Jah.* We'll see to it."

"And the cleaning and all?"

Matilda made a face. "You already told us all this, Sadie."

"I know. I worry."

"Well, don't. Lizzie and me will do everything."

"And I'll be back before you know it."

"Okay."

A van pulled into the drive and circled up to the porch. Sadie had already told everyone else good-bye, so she just gave Matilda one more hug and hurried down the steps. She put her bag in the van and just before she climbed inside, she turned back to the house to wave. She saw Lizzie standing at the front window, and she waved right along with Matilda.

Sadie got into her seat and pulled the van door closed. She fastened her seat belt, and they were off.

"I should have you there by noon," the driver said, glancing at her in his rearview mirror.

"That'll be fine," Sadie murmured, settling in for the ride.

As they left Hollybrook, Sadie tried to busy her mind with what she would cook for the Christmas meal. Of course, there would be no decorations to see to, unlike the *Englisch* homes around the area. Secretly, she always admired the flashing colorful lights that decorated *Englisch* homes. Sometimes, she could even see their Christmas trees through the windows, and they looked amazing all decorated and lit up.

She wondered what Peter would be eating for Christmas dinner. Would he be at his family's home or would he stay with the Gundys?

Ach. She'd better switch her mind to other things. Aaron

knew she was coming. Or he should—she'd written him the approximate time she'd be arriving. But then, she doubted he'd be there to greet her. All their meetings had been secret. She figured *Mammi* might have guessed they were seeing each other, but her grandmother wouldn't mention it.

She tried to relax. Tried to be excited about returning to Ainesburg. Wasn't that what she'd wanted all along? Then why did she feel empty inside? Where was the anticipation? She blew out her breath, disgusted with herself. What was wrong with her these days? She couldn't seem to manage her emotions at all.

Well, once she was back with her grandmother, that would change. She could sink back into her regular routine, if only for a few days. It would be a comfort, surely. Yes. Everything would be fine. Once she saw Aaron again, things would become clear. They could deepen their relationship and maybe even make plans for the future. Wouldn't her parents be happy for her if she revealed that she had a serious beau. A fine young man, too.

She clasped her hands tightly in her lap and pressed her lips into a fine line.

Everything was going to be fine, she told herself again.

Chapter Fourteen

Lizzie jumped on the bed, glad to be back in her own room. Surely, Sadie wouldn't mind if she slept in there while she was in Ohio. Lizzie flopped back, staring at the ceiling. It was a rare thing to have your own bedroom in an Amish home. There were usually too many children, and sharing was essential. But they were only five children at the Springer house, and with Sadie gone, only four. Of course, when the baby came, that would add another, but still, for now this bedroom was up for grabs.

Matilda had been offended when Lizzie told her she was going back to Sadie's room for the next few days. But that meant Matilda would have her own room, too, so there was no call to grumble. Matilda had drawn a picture for *Mammi* ... why hadn't Lizzie thought of that? It was a right kind thing to do.

Matilda was that way. She was nicer than Lizzie, more thoughtful. Lizzie frowned. Well, there was nothing stopping her from drawing a picture now and sending it by mail. She sat up and opened the bedside table drawer. She fished about inside for the tablet she knew was there.

She grabbed a handful of envelopes and pulled them out. They were addressed to Sadie, with no return. Her brow rose. A beau, perhaps? Her pulse increased, and she inspected the envelopes more carefully. Maybe, she should read one of the letters... Maybe, she should make sure that Sadie didn't need them in Ohio. She could always enclose them in a larger envelope and send them along with a drawing for *Mammi*.

Lizzie bit her lip. Sadie wouldn't need them. Who was she kidding? She just wanted an excuse to read them. Her fingers hovered over the first opened envelope. Curiosity burned through her. Was it a beau? And if so, who was he? Was he handsome? Tall or short?

Lizzie hesitated and then shame burned through her. She had no business prying into her sister's mail. She must not take out Sadie's personal letters and read them. That would be wrong. So very, very wrong.

With an exasperated moan, she replaced the envelopes in the drawer. She found the tablet and took it out. Then she stuck her hand back inside, digging around for a pen. Her hand felt a tightly folded wad of paper, and she took it out of the drawer. Strange. It was folded so small. Her curiosity now piqued beyond reason, she unfolded it.

It was a letter. *To Peter*. How strange...

Hardly knowing what she was doing, Lizzie read every word of it. By the time she finished, her eyes had misted over and her heart hurt. Poor Sadie. She loved Peter. Were the envelopes full of letters from Peter, then? She reached out to grab them and check, but she stopped herself. Reading a random piece of paper that was folded up was a far cry from opening a letter intentionally.

But why hadn't Sadie mailed this letter? It was clearly to Peter Wyse. In the letter, Sadie had said that Peter would never read it. Why? Didn't Sadie have an envelope and a stamp? Maybe she'd re-written the letter later and sent that copy instead. Maybe, she'd forgotten she'd written this one in the first place.

The letter nearly broke Lizzie's heart. Poor Sadie. She'd been so sad.

Lizzie stood up, making a decision. She could do this for Sadie. She could mail the letter for her. Sadie had done so many things for them these past days. Why, she'd worked herself to the bone taking care of all of them. This was something Lizzie could do for her. Excited now, she ran down the stairs, heading straight for the bureau where they kept a supply of envelopes and stamps.

Chapter Fifteen

"Child! You came!" *Mammi* exclaimed, holding out her arms. Sadie walked right into them, hugging her grandmother tightly.

"Hello, *Mammi*," she said, straightening back to her full height. "How are you?"

"Much better now you're here." *Mammi* wiped at the corners of her eyes. "You hungry?"

"I am." Sadie grinned. "Don't you fret. I know my way around your kitchen."

"That you do," *Mammi* said with a chuckle.

They both traipsed into the kitchen, where Sadie bustled about, getting a quick meal together.

Mammi sat down at the kitchen table, which Sadie found surprising. She sneaked a closer look at her grandmother's face. She looked tired. A sliver of fear lodged in Sadie's throat.

"Shall we eat in here or at the dining table?" she asked.

"In here is fine."

That was odd, too. Henrietta Verkler usually insisted that they sit at the dining table, even with only the two of them. Had something happened while Sadie was gone?

"All right," Sadie said, putting cheer into her voice. She set the food on the table and grabbed two plates and glasses and cutlery to set out. "Would you like milk? Or a cup of tea?"

"Milk's fine."

Sadie fetched the pitcher of milk and filled the glasses, then she sat at the table with her grandmother. *Mammi* led them in silent prayer, and they began eating. Sadie had a hard time concentrating on the food; her gaze kept going to her grandmother, trying to discern if something had changed.

"*Mammi*," she began and then paused. *Mammi* didn't take kindly to hints that she might be failing.

"*Jah?*" When Sadie didn't continue, *Mammi* put her thin hand on Sadie's arm. "What is it, child?"

Sadie shook her head. "Nothing, really." She took a deep breath. "Are you all right?"

Mammi's eyes filled with tears. "Of course, I'm all right," she snapped and blinked hard. "Why wouldn't I be?"

"*Mammi*, please..." Sadie let the words hang between them.

Finally, *Mammi* sighed and set down her fork. "Fine. You know me better than anyone, I s'pose. I been missing you is all."

Sadie clasped her grandmother's hand. "I've missed you, too."

Mammi looked down at her plate and Sadie could see that she wanted to say something more, and she was struggling with it. The seconds dragged out and Sadie held her breath.

"It ain't just missing you," *Mammi* continued, her voice hitching. "I been fretting."

"Fretting?"

"I-I, well, I never fretted about being alone before. But, but I have been of late."

Sadie jumped from her chair and went to her grandmother, putting her arms around Henrietta's thin shoulders. "*Ach, Mammi*. I don't like you being alone, either."

Mammi stiffened. "I can take care of myself."

"I know you can," Sadie was quick to say. "But it's much happier to live with someone, *ain't so*?"

Mammi's shoulders began to shake, and Sadie's eyes widened. Was she weeping? *Mammi* didn't weep. She was tough as nails.

"*Mammi*?" Sadie could hardly get the word out.

"Don't mind me," *Mammi* said, nearly pushing Sadie away. "I'm fine. I'm always fine."

Sadie slowly sat back down. She willed herself not to cry; *Mammi* wouldn't like it. She drew in a slow breath. "Maybe, we can talk about things tomorrow."

"What things would that be? You mean me leaving my home, don't you?" *Mammi* asked, but the edge was gone from her voice.

"Perhaps."

Mammi pursed her lips and scowled. She picked her fork back up, but before she took a bite, she muttered, "Fine. We'll talk tomorrow."

Chapter Sixteen

Peter looked at the envelope, turning it over and over in his hands. The handwriting looked like a child's, but what child would be writing him? After delivering the letter, Jess Gundy was still there, looking at him, as if waiting for Peter to open the letter in front of him—which he wasn't about to do.

"Thank you, Jess," Peter said again, palming the letter.

"All right, then." Jess turned to go and then hesitated. "The missus wants to know your plans for Christmas dinner," he continued. "Whether you'll be with us or with your folks."

Peter swallowed. "Likely with my folks, but thank you. I know I'm always welcome in your home."

"That you are. All right. Well, I'll get out of your hair." Jess raised his arm in a small wave and left the *daadi haus*.

Peter shut the door, eager to open the letter. He had no idea who had written it. At first, he'd dreamed it might be from Sadie, but he knew her penmanship from years before, and this wasn't hers. But who in the world would be writing to him? He stoked the warming stove and settled into the rocking chair. He carefully slid his finger under the flap, opening the envelope.

The letter had been folded and re-folded by the looks of it. He opened it and smoothed it out on his leg. His gaze dropped to the signature, and his breath caught. It *was* from Sadie... But the address had been written with another hand.

His eyes flew over the letter and his pulse increased with every line, until it was pounding against his ears. He stood and paced to the window and back. He reread every word.

Dear Peter,

I'm back in Hollybrook now. Of course, I don't expect you to know that, which is why I'm telling you. I didn't want to come. Because of you, Peter. Because of you. You hurt me so badly when you dropped me. I had thought that you liked me. Didn't you? How I liked you. Nee. How I loved you. You broke my heart.

When I look back now, I can still feel that young girl's broken heart. I don't really blame you, of course. You were totally free to choose whoever you wanted to court. I had hoped it would be me. And it was for a little while, wasn't it? I loved those times we spent together. I had such dreams. Oh, I was a foolish girl.

But I loved you.

I fear I still do. And I don't want to. You made your choice two years ago. So, loving you now is quite sad, actually. I am ashamed to even admit it, which is why I'm writing it in this letter which will never reach you.

I am so sorry for your loss, Peter. My heart breaks for you. How awful that Eloise died. I can't even imagine how hurt you must have been and maybe still are. She was a nice girl. But then, you know that. You loved her. I'm so sorry.

It's odd to be back home. I feel like time hasn't really passed. Like I'm caught in a spider web and can't pull myself out of it. I'm wriggling and wriggling, but I'm trapped in its sticky threads. I don't want to be here. I want to go back to Ohio to be with Mammi.

Yet part of me wants to see you first. Not necessarily to talk to you or anything, just to see you. I have such an image of you in my head, and I have no idea if you look the same or not. I don't even know if I look the same. Probably not. Two years can seem forever, can't it? Goodness. I just said the opposite earlier. I guess I just want to see if you're all right. I don't want to worry about you.

I don't want to think about you.

Maybe if I see you, I can forget you. And maybe if I see you, I won't feel anything. That's what I am hoping for. To not feel anything except Christian love.

Goodness, but I'm going on and on, aren't I? I guess it doesn't matter since you won't read this. So, really, I suppose I'm writing to myself. Now that is an odd thought.

Love,

Sadie

When had she written this? It sounded like she'd written it when she'd first returned. Why hadn't she sent it right away? And why did she say that he'd never read it? Hadn't she intended him to read it? And if not, why had she written it? It made no sense at all. He snatched up the envelope again, looking at the handwriting. Who'd addressed it? And why?

He let out a shaky breath. Wasn't he missing the point? Sadie loved him. She said so right there in her own words. She *loved him.* Tears sprang to his eyes and he found himself grinning. But if she loved him, why was she so bent on staying away from him? He glanced at the letter again.

Because she didn't trust him. She didn't know that he loved her right back.

And now she was gone. And she had a beau in Ohio—she'd told him as much. Were they together right that very minute? Were they planning a future together?

He couldn't abide the thought. Couldn't abide the thought of his beautiful Sadie with someone else. He should have made himself clear. Should have declared his feelings. He'd thought he had by placing his star stone in her pony cart. But she had given it back to him. Given it back. It didn't bear thinking about.

He grabbed his coat from its peg and left the house, the door slamming behind him. The phone shanty wasn't far. He could be there in under ten minutes.

Chapter Seventeen

Sadie combed her hair an extra fifty strokes. She carefully twisted it into a fresh bun at the back of her head. She put on her *kapp*, holding it firmly in place with bobby pins. She smoothed down her dress and then picked up the hand mirror from the dresser. Her cheeks were flushed which made her look either excited or fresh from the outdoors. But it was the look in her eyes that troubled her.

She was meeting Aaron in a few minutes. He'd left a note in *Mammi's* mailbox asking to see her on her first night back. She was glad because, in truth, he was one of the reasons she was there in the first place. But the look reflected in her eyes was wary. Almost frightened. But why? Aaron was a nice man, perfectly mannered and quite respectful. Why should she be afraid?

She pressed a hand to her chest. Because he was going to propose to her, that was why. She had no real proof that he would, but deep in her gut—and deep in her heart—she knew it was so. This was her moment. One that she had waited for ever since she was a young girl. Her romance was happening right now.

Oh, she wasn't so foolish as to think it would be accompanied by birds singing and sunshine floating down to kiss her brow, but she did hope it was special. Tender and moving.

Yet, all she felt was fright. Or foreboding. Or something. She couldn't quite pinpoint it. But the eager anticipation she hoped for had twisted into something not all that pleasant. Cold feet, she assumed. That was all it was.

If she married Aaron, she could stay right there in Ainesburg and *Mammi* could live with them. Or they with her, which would be even better. Of course, Sadie would have to go back to Hollybrook until her new sibling was born. And that was fine with her—she wanted to be of help.

She glanced at the wind-up clock on the dresser. Aaron would be waiting for her at the end of the drive any minute now. She left her room and went to tell her grandmother she was going out. When she entered the front room, she found *Mammi* sound asleep in the rocker, her head tilted to the side and her mouth slightly open, snoring softly.

Deciding against waking her up, Sadie quickly scribbled a note saying she was going out and set it on *Mammi's* lap. Then she bundled up and slipped out the door. Not surprisingly, Ohio was just as cold as Indiana. She sucked in her breath, lowered her head against the frigid air, and walked quickly across the lawn.

Aaron's buggy was already there. The passenger door swung open.

"Sadie! You're here!"

Sadie hurriedly got inside. With its heater, Aaron's buggy was pleasantly warm.

"Hello, Aaron."

"*Ach*, Sadie, it's *gut* to see you."

"It's *gut* to see you, too."

"I'm happy you're able to be here during Christmas. I bet your *mammi* is right glad."

"I think she is." Sadie searched his face, wondering if her guess had been right. Was he going to speak about their future together?

"Let's get going," Aaron said, slapping the reins. The buggy rocked into motion, rolling at a brisk clip down the road.

Sadie's chest felt tight, and she had to force herself to take even breaths. Aaron was safe to her. Familiar. Kind. She tried to relax. He must have felt her studying him because he turned to her and grinned. He reached out and took her hand in his.

"I'm so happy to be here with you," he said. He inched closer, and she had a sudden thought that he might lean over and kiss her cheek. She had no idea how she felt about that. He'd never kissed her before, and she'd never been kissed by any boy, not even Peter.

The buggy hit a sizeable rock or something hard in the worn grooves on the asphalt, because it lurched and Aaron dropped her hand and put his full attention back on driving. He laughed. "Sorry about that. Something in the road I guess."

"No harm done." Sadie swallowed with difficulty and focused her gaze on the road before them, too.

"How is your *mamm*?"

"She's doing all right. Resting a lot. My sisters are going to help with everything until I return."

"That's *gut*." He sighed audibly. "Uh, Sadie? Will you be staying in Indiana when you go back?"

She turned to look at him again. "I don't know for sure." Was this it? Was he about to ask her? Was her future about to be sealed?

"I'm hoping you'll come back here." His hands were shaking —she was sure of it. He continued. "I'm hoping you'll have a big reason for coming back..."

She held her breath.

"Sadie, I'm twenty-three years old. I don't know if you knew that. I'm ready to settle down."

She tensed.

"I am wondering if, well, if you'd like to become even more serious. Truth be told, I'm thinking of a possible future together." He was so nervous, that Sadie wanted to squirm. "Would you... I mean, could you consider marrying me?"

And there it was. Sadie blinked rapidly and opened her mouth. The word *yes* hovered on her tongue, but nothing came out. Not one sound. Horrified, she clamped her lips together. What was happening? This was *it*. The moment she'd waited for all her life. The moment every Amish girl waited for.

"Sadie?" There was a note of panic in his voice.

She forced her lips open. "I-I..."

And visions of Peter flooded her mind. Visions of him years ago—his smile, his laughter when he'd cracked a good joke, the twinkle in his eye when he gazed at her. And visions of him now—the earnest expression when he looked at her, his bitter disappointment when she'd handed his stone back to him. The images flipped through her mind. Peter in his straw hat; Peter in his felt hat; Peter walking toward her, Peter walking away from her.

She gasped and wanted to sob out the futility of it. She had no business being there with Aaron. He was a good man, and he deserved someone who loved him. Truly loved him.

"I-I'm so sorry," she stammered. "Take me home, Aaron. I'm so so sorry."

His expression was as if she'd struck him. "But I don't understand—"

"I know. I'm sorry. Please, Aaron. Take me back home." She was crying then, tears streaming down her face.

"But Sadie—"

She turned away, pressing her cheek against the frame of the door. How had she let it go this far? She was now hurting Aaron just as Peter had hurt her. She felt miserable. Miserable and guilty. When Aaron stopped to let her out, she turned to him.

"You're a wonderful man, Aaron. I'm just not the right girl for you." She opened the door, nearly tripping in her haste to get away.

She cried all the way back to the house.

Chapter Eighteen

Mammi wouldn't stop staring at her. Sadie could feel her eyes penetrate her back as she went about preparing breakfast. Finally, she couldn't take it anymore.

Whirling around, she asked, "What is it?"

Mammi's eyes narrowed. "What's wrong with you this morning?"

Sadie sighed, sinking into the nearest kitchen chair. "I went out last night."

"I know that. You left me a note. I didn't hear you come in, though. What happened?"

"I, well, I cut things off with a young man last night."

Mammi inhaled sharply. "Did you now?"

"*Jah.*"

"But you ain't happy about it?"

"It had to be done."

"Why?" *Mammi* asked and then dawning came over her face. "*Ach*... You fancy someone else."

Sadie sighed.

"I see." *Mammi* walked over to her and put her hands on Sadie's shoulders. "The Lord *Gott* will work things out, child. Have no doubt of that."

Sadie nodded and stood. "Maybe. In the meantime, let me get breakfast on the table." She went back to moving about the kitchen, frying eggs and flipping the potato cakes.

She was relieved that she'd broken things off with Aaron. She only prayed that he wasn't too badly hurt. Of course, her thoughts kept circling back to Peter, but she'd done a pretty complete job of blocking any future with him. Why had she been so cold to him? So unforgiving?

Fear.

Plain and simple, she was afraid of being hurt again. So afraid, though, that she cut off any possibility of being with the man she truly loved? Annoyed with herself, she scrambled the eggs too vigorously, slopping big chunks onto the cooking stove.

Mammi was at her elbow, chuckling now. "Sit down, child. I'll finish up."

Sadie handed her the spatula.

"I don't s'pose you'd like to tell me who it is you're pining after."

"I don't suppose I would," Sadie said, giving her grandmother a sheepish smile.

"At least, you're smiling now." *Mammi* finished up the eggs and turned off the burner. "Bring me them plates, will you?"

Sadie did, and within minutes, they were sitting together eating. When they were finished, Sadie insisted that she *red* up the kitchen alone. *Mammi* didn't argue and headed off toward the front room.

A knock sounded on the front door.

"I'll get it," *Mammi* called.

Sadie began filling the sink with water to wash the dishes when she heard *Mammi* clear her throat behind her. She turned and dropped the two dirty forks she was holding. They clattered to the floor at her feet.

"What are you doing here?" she cried, her heart pounding wilding.

"I came to see you," Peter said. He held a crumpled letter out for her to see.

"What?" Sadie pressed herself against the counter. She stared unbelievingly at the letter she'd hidden in her bedside table. "How did you get that?"

"You wrote this, didn't you?"

Mammi pushed around Sadie to turn the faucet off. Then she disappeared from the kitchen.

"I-I did. But how in the world did you get it?"

"I don't know." He then held the envelope toward her. "It came in this."

Sadie gasped, recognizing Lizzie's handwriting. *Ach!* Wait till she got ahold of the girl.

"Did you mean it?" Peter asked. "What you wrote?"

She looked into his eyes and saw something akin to desperation. He wanted her to mean it. He wanted it to be true.

"I meant it," she whispered.

"Sadie." That was all. Just her name. But it held everything. It held a promise so big and so beautiful that it encompassed her entire world. "Sadie." He said her name again, and it was like a caress on her wounded heart.

Her throat tightened until she could hardly draw a breath. "Peter?" she uttered back, her voice choked.

And then he crossed the room and took her into his arms. He

held her to his chest and she felt his heart beating wildly against her cheek. "Sadie, I love you. I love you, Sadie."

"B-but..." Sadie stuttered, hardly daring to believe his words—hardly daring to believe what was happening.

He drew back, and his eyes were full of understanding. "I know you're having trouble believing me after how I acted before..."

She blinked, willing herself not to cry.

"I did love you, Sadie. Not as much as I do now, but I did. I'm sorry I hurt you. I can't even give you a decent explanation for what happened. When Eloise, well, when she took notice of me... I-I'm sorry. I don't want to hurt you anymore than I already have."

"I want to hear," she said, bracing herself. "I want to hear what you have to say."

He looked hesitant and reluctant, but he continued. "She needed me, Sadie. She *needed* me. There was something about her, something fragile and weak. I let it go straight to my heart. I wanted to protect her." He shook his head. "I don't know if I can explain it proper-like. And I did love her. When she died..."

He stopped then and took a huge breath. "When she died, my world stopped. Everything seemed to die with her. But as time went on, as I began to live again, I found myself yearning for you."

Sadie's eyes brimmed with tears. His words squeezed her heart, but she had to hear them. She had to know.

"It was odd, Sadie. After she died, I missed Eloise so much. And I still miss her. I suppose maybe I always will. But my heart..." He shook his head again and gave Sadie such a look of desperation that she could barely draw breath. "My heart, so *much* of my heart, Sadie, has always been yours. I can't stop thinking about you. I want to be with you. I want to tell you things all day long. I want to hear your laughter, see your smile. I want... Sadie, I want you."

Her heart hammered against her chest. She put her hand to her throat, and his words whirled through her mind.

"Sadie, I know you don't trust me, and I don't blame you. But if you could try... If you could at least try to trust me again... I want us to be together. I want to court you. I want us to be married."

She was openly crying now. She gazed up at him through her tears, and the love she'd always had for him swelled within her until she could barely swallow. She loved him. Oh, *how she loved him*. She'd never stopped loving him.

He took her in his arms again and bent his head over her and covered the top of her *kapp* with kisses. She tightened her arms around him, and he moaned into her hair. They stood there for a long time, pressed tightly against each other. She breathed him in, breathed in the smell of soap and shampoo and hay and cold outdoors. She closed her eyes, burying her face into his chest, still feeling his heart beating, timing her breathing to his.

Finally, he loosened his grip and she gazed up at him, at his beautiful face, at his blue eyes that looked almost purple, at his mouth smiling down at her.

"Could you, Sadie? Could you possibly agree to marry me?"

Her breath caught and she nodded. "I'll marry you," she said, biting back a sob of joy.

He closed his eyes and whispered his thanks to God.

She took his hand and squeezed it, feeling his strength and his love. She swallowed and licked her lips. "I'm going to talk *Mammi* into moving to Hollybrook," she said in a whisper.

"I thought she wouldn't go."

"Something has changed. I think she'll go this time."

Peter bent down and kissed her cheek, his lips lingering on her skin. "She can live with us," he whispered back. "We'll celebrate next Christmas together."

Sadie nearly cried out with happiness. She had never loved Peter more than she did that very moment.

There was a noise from the doorway. "I'll stay with my son and his wife, thank you anyway," came *Mammi's* voice.

Sadie twirled around to look at her. "So, you *will* come, *Mammi*?"

Her grandmother nodded, though there was sorrow in her eyes. "I'll come. It's time. I can't pretend anymore."

"Everyone will be so glad," Sadie said.

"All right, enough about me," Mammi said, taking another step into the room. "Now are you going to introduce me proper to your young man?"

All three of them laughed, and Sadie made the "proper" introductions with complete pleasure.

The End

Continue Reading...

Thank you for reading ***Christmas in Hollybrook!*** **Are you wondering what to read next?** Why not read ***The Stepmother*****. Here's a sample for you:**

Rebecca bustled from the kitchen, balancing a platter of freshly-sliced homemade bread and two glasses filled with cold milk. She put them on the table and ran back for the other glasses of milk. When she'd gotten them plunked down, sloshing only a little, she stood back and surveyed her work.

Seven places set. Everything ready—except the large pot of stew, which she didn't want to take from the cooking stove until the van arrived. She bit the corner of her lip. Everything had to be perfect. She ran into the bathroom at the back of the house and peered into the small mirror above the sink.

Her cheeks were flushed bright red, and no matter how she

tried to hide it, her eyes revealed her nervousness. She tried on a smile, but it looked as if she'd plastered it on with a knife. She took a huge, gulping breath and tried again. No. The smile was no good. She made a face into the mirror, and then chastised herself for being so proud as to be standing there practicing a smile. Goodness, when had she become so vain?

She turned away and went to the side door of the house, opening it and pushing the screen door to stick her head outside. The air nipped at her, but being only November, it hadn't grown too cold yet.

"Stephen! Stephen, come on in!" she hollered to her older brother. Stephen was married with a wife and baby daughter, but he'd traveled that day from Illinois to show his support to their father. Tabitha had stayed behind with little Nessy who had the sniffles.

Stephen emerged from the barn, wiping his hands on an old towel. "They're not here," he called back to her.

"Any minute now." She glanced toward the gravel drive which as of yet was completely empty of a van. But her father had sent word that they would be arriving shortly after noon that day. And when Rebecca had checked, it was already seven minutes after twelve.

Stephen walked over to her and clutched the handle of the screen. "You're nervous," he stated and then pushed past her into the house.

She followed him. "I know. I can't help it. We don't even know her, Stephen. What if I don't like her?"

He raised a brow. "You'll like her. If *Dat* liked her enough to marry her, then she has to be all right, *ain't so?*"

Rebecca shrugged. Maybe or maybe not.

"And three sons. Think on it. This house is going to be full," she continued.

Stephen gave her a strange look. "Three sons ain't nothing. What ails you? You're jumpier than I thought."

Rebecca stared at her brother, annoyed. "Wouldn't you be? What if it was you welcoming our new stepmother into your home? What if you were welcoming three new stepbrothers to live with you?" Rebecca glanced around the house. "I've been taking care of everything for as long as I can remember around here. It's going to be awful different."

Her voice faltered, and she swallowed back the sudden tears clogging her throat.

Her brother put his hand on her shoulder. "Ever think that maybe this is a *gut* thing? Ever think that maybe things will be better now?"

She blinked and tried to swallow. Her brother was right. Where was her faith? Where was her confidence in her dad? She shuddered and squared her shoulders.

"Lands sake, why are we standing around like fence posts

anyway? I need to get the pot of stew on the table. You wash up."

She turned on her heel and fairly marched into the kitchen. *My kitchen,* she thought ruefully and pressed her lips together. Enough of that. Her dad was counting on her. She grabbed two hot pads and lifted the kettle from the cooking stove, walking carefully to the table with it. Even if the van didn't arrive from Linnow Creek for another fifteen minutes, the stew would surely hold its heat. She'd made it extra careful that day, cutting large chunks of stew meat, and not even thinking of conserving when she'd cut up potatoes and onions and carrots and emptied canned veggies into the stock.

She froze. *"Ach, nee!"*

Stephen poked his head out from the wash room. "What is it? What's happened?"

"I forgot to make the cornbread! Now, the meal is ruined! How in the world could I have forgotten?"

She threw the hot pads onto her plate and dashed back into the kitchen, whirling through the room, snatching ingredients from all the shelves. What was wrong with her? She always served up cornbread with stew. Her dad loved it and *expected* it. She ran to the gas fridge and grabbed three eggs. She closed the door with her hip and hurried to the counter.

"It ain't the end of the world, you know," Stephen said dryly from the door.

"No, it ain't, but *Dat* will be wondering at me. Wondering where my head is!"

She hurriedly began measuring out the ingredients, stirring like there was no tomorrow.

"*Ach.* The cooking stove."

Just then, the crunch of gravel was heard in the driveway. Rebecca crossed to the window and peered out. Sure enough, it was their regular Mennonite driver with his van, pulling in with a full load of passengers.

"Too late now," Stephen said. "Come on, Rebecca. Don't fret. Let's go meet our new family."

Rebecca stood very still. They had arrived. For six months, her dad had been traveling back and forth to Linnow Creek, courting the widow Amelia. Not once had Rebecca met her. She hadn't even traveled to Linnow Creek for the wedding. Her father had told her that she couldn't leave her goats that long. Nor the rest of the animals. In truth, his willingness to cut her out of the celebration hurt.

Why couldn't they have gotten their neighbors to watch the goats—to milk them and feed them? And the chickens and the cow and horses? It would have only been for a night or two. The Guths down the road would have been happy to oblige, but Rebecca hadn't pushed it. She'd been so stunned by her father's attitude that she had just nodded and gone along with it.

Now, she regretted it. She should have insisted on joining her dad—but a daughter insisting something contrary to her father's wishes wasn't done.

Stephen and his wife had been all right with missing the ceremony. Neither he nor his wife had been inclined to take a trip with their five-month-old baby. Stephen was content with just coming to Hollybrook alone and meeting Amelia and her boys here.

And her brother Amos?

Rebecca swallowed past the sudden lump in her throat. Amos was a different story entirely. Her heart gave its usual lurch at the thought of her lost brother.

"You coming?" Stephen asked.

Rebecca gave a start and shook herself from her thoughts. "*Jah, jah*. Of course."

CLICK HERE To Read More of *The Stepmother:*

http://ticahousepublishing.com/amish.html

Thank you for Reading

If you **love Amish Romance**, **Visit Here:**

http://ticahousepublishing.subscribemenow.com

to find out about all **New Hollybrook Amish Romance Releases! We will let you know as soon as they become available!**

If you enjoyed ***Christmas in Hollybrook!*** would you kindly take a couple minutes to leave a positive review on Amazon? It only takes a moment, and positive reviews truly make a difference. I would be so grateful! Thank you!

Turn the page to discover more Amish Romances just for you!

More Amish Romance for You

We love clean, sweet, rich Amish Romances and have a lovely library of Brenda Maxfield titles just for you! If you love bargains, you may want to start right here! Here is a sampling of our BARGAIN Box Sets!

Amish Romance Bundle
Living Hope
BRENDA MAXFIELD
Replacement Wife
The Promise
The Wedding
Mellie's Sweet Shop
Leaving Hollybrook
The Fire
The Amish Blogger
Missing Mama
The Big Freeze

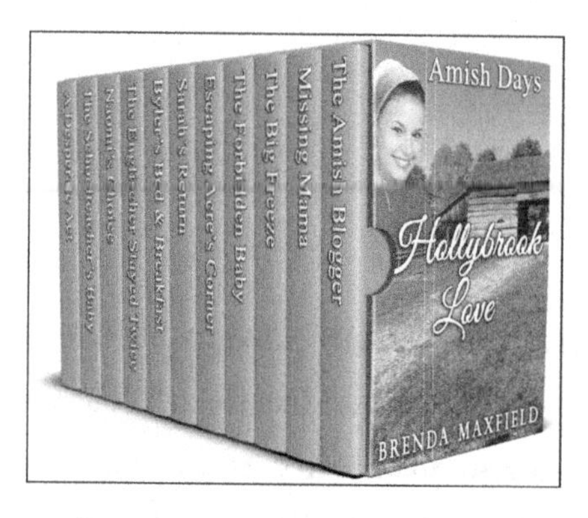
Amish Days
Hollybrook Love
BRENDA MAXFIELD
The Amish Blogger
Missing Mama
The Big Freeze
The Forbidden Baby
Escaping Acre's Corner
Sarah's Return
Byler's Bed & Breakfast

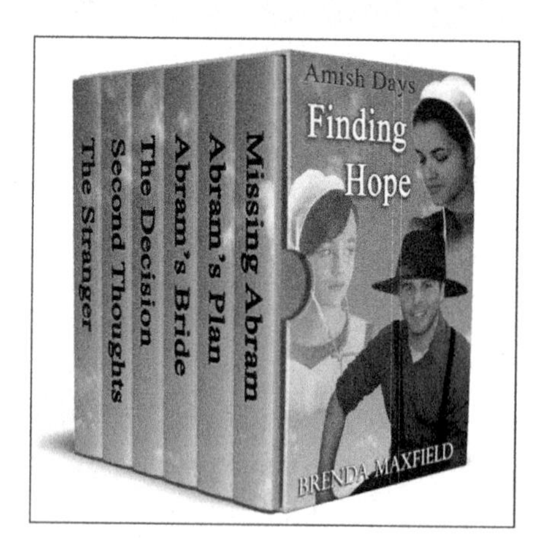
Amish Days
Finding Hope
BRENDA MAXFIELD
Missing Abram
Abram's Plan
Abram's Bride
The Decision
Second Thoughts
The Stranger

Find our complete list of box sets here:

http://ticahousepublishing.com/bargains-amish-box-sets.html

Here is the list of Brenda's single titles. They are conveniently grouped by our lovely Amish heroines. You're sure to find many favorites. Enjoy!

Hope's Story

Missing Abram

Abram's Plan

Abram's Bride

Sally's Story

The Decision

Second Thoughts

The Stranger

The Runaway

Josie's Story

The Schoolteacher's Baby

A Desperate Act

Marian's Story

The Amish Blogger

Missing Mama

The Big Freeze

A Loving Stranger

Annie's Story

The Forbidden Baby

Escaping Acre's Corner

Sarah's Return

Naomi's Story

Byler's Bed & Breakfast

The Englischer Stayed Twice

Naomi's Choice

Mellie's Story

Mellie's Sweet Shop

Leaving Hollybrook

The Fire

Faith's Story

The Adoption

Changing her Mind

Home at Last

Rhoda's Story

The Amish Beekeeper

The Accident

Coming Home

Greta's Story

Replacement Wife

The Promise

The Wedding

Nancy's Story

The Mother's Helper

Losing Ariel

A Question of Faith

Elsie's Story

Helping Mammi

Amish Imposter

Choosing Amish

Mary's Story

Broken Promises

The Loss

The Restoration

Tessa's Story

The Lie

Tessa's Baby

The Truth

Ruby's Story

Separated

The Option

Together at Last

Emma's Story

The Deacon's Son

The Defiance

Emma's Decision

Rebecca's Story

The Stepmother

The Search

Meeting Amos

http://ticahousepublishing.com/amish.html

About the Author

My passion is writing! What could be more delicious than inventing new characters and seeing where they take you?

I am blessed to live in Indiana, a state I share with many Amish communities. (I find the best spices, hot cereal, and good cooking advice at an Amish store not too far away.)

I've lived in Honduras, Grand Cayman, and Costa Rica. One of my favorite activities is exploring other cultures. My husband, Paul, and I have two grown children and five precious grandchildren, three, special delivery from Africa and two, homegrown. I love to hole up in our lake cabin and write -- often with a batch of popcorn nearby. (Oh, and did I mention dark chocolate?)

I enjoy getting to know my readers, so feel free to write me at: contact@brendamaxfield.com. Subscribe to my Newsletter and get the latest news about releases:

http://ticahousepublishing.subscribemenow.com

Happy Reading!

www.ticahousepublishing.com
contact@brendamaxfield